THE AMATEUR ACTOR

by

FRANCES MACKENZIE

M.B.E., M.A. (OXON.)

FORMERLY PRINCIPAL OF THE TRAINING DEPARTMENT
THE BRITISH DRAMA LEAGUE

THEATRE ARTS BOOKS
NEW YORK

THIS THIRD EDITION PUBLISHED BY
THEATRE ARTS BOOKS
333 SIXTH AVENUE
NEW YORK 10014
IN 1966
SECOND PRINTING 1968

PRINTED IN GREAT BRITAIN BY
THE BOWERING PRESS
PLYMOUTH

Library of Congress Catalog Card No. 66–24456

©

FRANCES MACKENZIE
1966

FIRST PUBLISHED BY THOMAS NELSON AND SONS LTD
IN AUGUST 1935
REVISED AND ENLARGED EDITION JANUARY 1936
REPRINTED 1945 (TWICE), 1947, 1949, 1954, 1958

NOTE

Throughout this book the terms "left" and "right," applied to the stage, refer to the actor's left or right as he faces the audience. "Up stage" denotes the back of the stage, and "down stage" the front of the stage.

Note for the American Edition: In the theatre language of Great Britain the word "producer" refers to the person who in the United States is called a "director". And the British equivalent of the U.S. "producer" is a "manager". Since this book was written in England, it was thought wise to leave these terms as they were in the author's manuscript.

THB EDITOR

CONTENTS

APPENDIX

EXERCISES

CHAPTER I

WHITHER THE AMATEUR?

THOSE of us—and we are many—who take an active interest in amateur acting are beginning to ask ourselves: What is the future of the amateur dramatic movement? What stage has it reached, and what stage can it reach?

Every one will readily admit that amateur drama has achieved a level of efficiency which is as far removed from Edwardian "amateur theatricals" as is present-day club tennis from Edwardian garden-party tennis.

No longer is it considered "fun" to put on a play of which the successful performance is a miracle of good luck; in which none of the actors knows a word of his part; the inexperienced lose their heads and giggle, while the old hands gag shamelessly; the curtain rises late and descends early—owing to a broken rope; intervals are long, and relieved only by the sound of bumps and whispered execrations from behind the curtain; the play drags on its weary way, enlivened spasmodically by an outburst of excessive brightness from the leading lady or gentleman. Yet, at the end, the audience starts from its slumber to applaud vociferously; the stage is transformed into a catafalque of floral tributes—even the prompter is not forgotten; the show is "glorious fun" and "a huge success", and the leading lady is "a born actress and ought to take it up professionally".

All that is of the past. The amateur of today has developed not only an artistic conscience, but a conscience towards his public. He would consider it disgraceful to put on a show in which the actors did not know their

1

lines or were inaudible, and in which hitches, delays, and a shapeless performance exhausted the patience or insulted the intelligence of his audience. He takes trouble; he invites serious criticism; and he seeks instruction. The public, too, is gradually beginning to take him seriously.

These improvements, however, are more strikingly manifest in the production and presentation of plays than in the acting. While the standard of production is frequently satisfactory, and in many cases reaches a level of considerable artistic achievement, the acting, for the most part, seldom gets beyond a certain degree of competence.

Looking back upon a large number of amateur performances and dramatic festivals witnessed during the past few years, one can recall much that was good and interesting in production, beautiful settings, and effective lighting, but the general impression left by the acting is one of rather dreary uniformity. It is indefinite, anaemic, and lacking in personality and vitality. Perhaps in one play out of ten one would see a clear-cut, vigorous, and sensitive performance which would shine out like a beacon in a murky sea of gentility.

It would appear in so many dramatic societies that all the intelligence of the company is concentrated upon the production and presentation, while the actor is left to flounder.

There is a serious danger, both in the amateur and professional theatre of the more experimental type, of magnifying the importance of the producer's work at the expense of the acting. Good acting is an essential part of good production, and the producer who neglects the individual acting of his company is defeating his own ends.

It is significant that in some counties where serious dramatic work has been going on for some years the standard of acting—if county festivals can be considered fairly representative—is no higher than in counties which are holding their first festival, and in which there has been practically no previous experience of acting.

Does this mean that amateur acting can never hope to advance beyond a certain point? If so, the future of the amateur dramatic movement would be barren indeed. One cannot believe that this is so. It does mean, however, that something must be done to bring the quality of acting up to the level of that of production.

What the amateur most sorely needs, if he is to improve, is more opportunity for practice and instruction. After all, the main difference between the amateur and the professional is that of experience and training. The amateur actor must try to learn his job, and in this he should receive more help from his producer. The producer is often exasperated by the inability of his actors to get the effects he wants, and which he sees so clearly in his own mind, but he does not always realize that it is his own inability to help and instruct his actors that is the cause of the trouble. Coaching which merely takes the form of destructive criticism is more of a hindrance than a help. The amateur producer, unlike the professional, is dealing with inexperienced actors, and he has to train them in their job as he goes along. This is not easy, but it is as important a part of his work as producer as is the creation of form and atmosphere and the representation of the author's intention in a play.

The suggestions in the following chapters are offered in the hope that they may be of use to those actors whose time affords them little opportunity for the necessary practice, and possibly, also, to help producers who find difficulty in helping their actors.

The book is intended to be a practical handbook for

the inexperienced amateur, and a large part of its material has been suggested by problems and difficulties that have arisen during rehearsals or classes. It is not within its scope to enter into the more profound aspects of the art of acting, or to deal with its finer points, or with related subjects, such as costume and make-up. Its purpose is to encourage the beginner to take his acting seriously, and he will then wish to explore the subject further in such books as Coquelin's *The Art of the Actor*, Stanislavsky's *An Actor Prepares*, and other works which are mentioned in the bibliography at the end of this book.

CHAPTER II

THE ACTOR'S APPROACH TO HIS ART

A PROFESSIONAL actress was recently glancing at the programme of a drama school for amateurs when her eye was caught by an item: "Class in Acting." She exclaimed: "How on earth can you teach people to act? Either you can act, or you can't."

That, of course, is one of the chief differences between the professional and the amateur. Broadly speaking, the professional does not act unless he can, while the amateur does, although he can't. Nothing will stop him.

None the less, it is not entirely true to say that you cannot teach a person to act, because there is, after all, no such thing as a "born actor". True, the gift and instinct for acting must be born, but the actor must be made by the sweat of his brow, and there is perhaps some consolation in the thought that although a *great* actor must be born, a competent actor can be made.

The professional actor learns to act by doing it; by constant practice, and an ever-increasing accumulation of experience. The amateur never gets this opportunity. He seldom plays in a production that runs longer than a week. More often he plays for only one or two performances, and probably he does not play more than half a dozen parts in a year at the most. He cannot, therefore, learn his art by practising it. He is obliged to seek other means. He must substitute short cuts for experience; attend classes, study textbooks.

If what follows appears merely to skim over the surface of a vast subject, it may at least serve as a warning to the hardy amateur who is beguiled into acting because he thinks it is easy.

It is only comparatively recently that the amateur has come to realize that acting is an art that must be studied in the same way as any other art. There are still many people —leaders of social organizations particularly—who, while admitting that for such activities as singing, drawing, handicrafts, or dancing, some preliminary instruction is necessary, cannot see that the same applies to acting, and will plunge blithely into dramatic production.

The word "technique" in connection with amateur acting should be used with discretion, as it so often appears to fill people with alarm. At the mention of the word they will exclaim: "Oh, but we don't want anything so advanced as that. We just act because we enjoy it."

Why do we Act?

This brings us to the crux of the whole matter. We act because we enjoy it, but *why* do we enjoy it? It is important to analyse one's motives in acting in order to discover from what angle we are approaching our art.

The only adequate answer to the question, "Why do you act?" is "Because I must", and no one who cannot give this as his only answer should dream of making acting his career. But in the case of the amateur it is different. He has many other answers.

These may be:

(*a*) Because it is fun. (Personal reasons.)

(*b*) Because it is a Good Thing. (Social or educational reasons.)

(*c*) To oblige. (Coercion.)

For the moment we need only concern ourselves with those whose answer is (*a*), while (*b*) have our respect, and (*c*) our sympathy.

We act because it is fun, because we enjoy it, but it is not easy always to say precisely in what our enjoyment lies in acting, as there are so many different aspects of it, each with a rather different appeal. Perhaps we may enjoy—somewhat vaguely—the sensation of "expressing ourselves", particularly some part of ourselves which is normally repressed. Better still, we enjoy being taken right out of ourselves and being, for a time, someone entirely different, as far removed as possible from our everyday selves. The childish instinct of "make-believe" is still strong in most of us, and is, in varying degrees, a powerful creative force.

Again, though few of us would admit it, our enjoyment may be entirely dependent on the stimulus of an audience; the thrill of appearing on a brightly lighted stage, wearing becoming costume and make-up, at our best, with the eyes and ears of a crowd of expectant people, dimly discerned beyond the glare of the footlights, watching and listening to us, wishing us well. This feeling, though probably to a great extent subconscious, is really the motive force of a large percentage of acting, both amateur and professional. It is natural and legitimate, and a certain element of self-exhibitionism is desirable in the actor: frequently, in the case of the highly intelligent, over-modest amateur, one could wish for more of it. But in itself it is not sufficient, and it behoves us all, at an early stage in our acting career, to be honest with ourselves, and to analyse our motives if we want to make sure whether we are really potential artists or merely exhibitionists.

The exhibitionist in us is easily tested. If we find that, after one or two gratifyingly successful performances, our next performance is not quite so successful and consequently our interest and enjoyment begin to flag; if we fail to find any pleasure in playing difficult, unattractive, or small parts, then, if we are honest, we will throw in our hand and confess that our interest is not in acting at all, but in self-exploitation.

This conclusion can only be reached after some experience; but if, having reached it, actors would desist from acting, we should be so much the nearer to building up real theatre in our midst.

The need for Technique

Let us assume, then, that we have satisfactorily refuted the charge of exhibitionism; that we find our interest increases with our difficulties, and that wrestling with uncongenial parts is stimulating. What then? We are perhaps on the way to becoming creative artists, but are we getting our full measure of enjoyment out of the process? Not always. We have grown criticial of our own efforts, and they do not satisfy us. We are constantly baffled by the consciousness that the idea formed so clearly in our imagination is failing to find expression in our performance. We are not "getting over" the effect we intend; we do not know how to bridge the gulf between our mind and that of the audience. In a word, we lack technique. Technique is simply the means, or instrument, by which the actor expresses his conception of a character so that it is communicated to the audience. The actor strives to create, or interpret, with truth, and to communicate with clarity. Therefore he must acquire some mastery of his instrument, i.e. his voice and body. To any artist an idea conceived but unable to find expression is torment, while the consciousness of having found the right means of expression is ecstasy. We may know the exasperation of hearing a phrase of music sing and flow in our head, to be defeated by the stumbling clumsiness of our own fingers on the keys when we attempt to reproduce the passage; or we may see clearly the strong, flowing curves of a human figure in motion, and be able to reproduce on paper only a shapeless wavering caricature of it. It is the same in acting. So often, at a performance, we suddenly hear our own voice saying a sentence in a certain way, and are quite startled to realize that it was not in the least how we intended it to sound. It is only at those rare moments, when we feel our technique respond to the call of our imagination, that we get the fullest thrill of enjoyment from our acting. That enjoyment is so intense that it is worth the pedestrian strivings and the cold-blooded analysis through which we have had to go in order to win it.

This business of acquiring technique is not, after all, so formidable, and the actor can do a great deal towards training himself. He will probably go through alternating stages of exaltation and depression, something like those of a person beginning to play golf. Many people will take an infinity of pains to acquire this hobby, which they would grudge to the hobby of acting.

Three Stages

The first stage of the would-be golfer is enlivened by "beginner's luck". The enthusiast goes out with club and ball for the first time, and achieves amazing results. Though there are occasional misses, quite often the ball goes soaring delightfully through the air, and he thinks: "This is easy; there is nothing in it. I've evidently got the knack of it". Next day, however, the misses are more frequent, and the good shots very rare. "Not so good", he says. "I must have some lessons."

Then comes the second, laborious stage, wherein the student is overwhelmed by the undreamt-of technical subtleties which are revealed to him by his teacher. In his efforts to remember the correct grip; the correct stance; to keep his eye on the ball; not to overswing; to follow through; to keep his head steady and his shoulders loose —he completely loses the thrill of that first carefree day when he hit the ball well and truly, without taking thought. He feels there is so much to learn that he begins to despair, and may give up, defeated.

If, however, he has enough of the British bulldog in him, he may win through to the third and final stage in which all these things, which caused him so much anguish to rmember, have become subconscious, and now he can be fairly sure of getting not one brilliant shot to ten misses, but two or three brilliant shots to ten good ones.

In just the same way the amateur actor may begin by giving a brilliant performance, and, encouraged by the congratulations of his friends, he thinks it is easy to act. Some time later he gives a second performance—possibly of the same play—and is dismayed to find that he can in no measure recapture the inspiration of that first dazzling night when he felt like a god suddenly made free of some new heaven. He no longer walks on air; he is conscious of his body, particularly of his hands. He hears his voice sounding sharp and dry through nervousness. He is conscious of the audience; of their restlessness. That "something" that seemed to guide him before, and direct his every action, is no longer there. He is definitely "not in the mood". He decides that acting is not always easy. He seeks instruction.

He then arrives at Stage Two, when he goes through a difficult period of acute self-consciousness. He is trying to control the inflections of his voice and the poise of his body, and he can no longer lose himself in his part. There are so many things to remember. But at this difficult stage he must bear in mind that the very fact that he has become critically conscious of his own efforts is in itself a sign of grace. Too many amateurs are content to trust to luck and the inspiration of the moment, and though they may achieve an occasional flash-in-the-pan success, they have no idea how they obtained their effects, and no assurance of being able to repeat them.

It is during this second stage of study and experiment that the actor must beware of getting into bad habits, and of receiving the wrong sort of instruction. He may develop artificial tricks of speech, irritating mannerisms, meaningless movements, and, worse, a habit of playing consciously and obviously to the audience, which will later become so much a part of his acting that he cannot rid himself of them.

If, however, he studies with intelligence, he will very soon assimilate enough technique to give him a certain amount of ease in performance. Control of speech and movement will become subconscious, and the enjoyment of losing himself in his part will return, greatly intensified by his command of his means of expression. He will have laid the foundation on which to build up his experience.

CHAPTER III

THE ACTOR'S APPROACH TO HIS PART

There are no Rules

IT is well to bear in mind that there are no hard and fast rules in acting, or in any other art. People tend to ask for dicta to be given them in black and white, in order to save them the trouble of thinking for themselves. They will say, for example, "But I thought it was a *rule* that you must never speak with your back to the audience," or, "I thought you must *never* cross in front of a person on the stage." Although eight times out of ten it might be wrong to do these things, twice out of ten times it would be absolutely right. There are no rules which cannot be broken.

There are hundreds of different ways of studying a part, and different temperaments are helped by different things. What follow are only suggestions which are the outcome of a pooling of experience.

Study the Whole Play

The actor should always be given the opportunity of reading the whole play at the outset, before he begins to study his own part, even if it is a minor one. It is a deplorable practice to give the actor only a script of his own lines, with a word or two of cue, so that he has no idea what the play is about, nor how much of the play happens between his speeches, until he comes to rehearsal. It encourages him to think only of his own part, and makes it impossible for him to understand the form and balance of the play as a whole.

In the case of an unpublished play it is sometimes difficult to provide a large number of copies of the complete script, but it should be possible to call the company together to read the play through, or to hear it read. Amateurs, however, more often work from published plays, in which case there is no excuse for lack of copies. After a preliminary reading, the actor ought to be sufficiently interested to wish to buy a copy of the play for himself, in which he can make his own notes.

<u>First</u> of all, then, <u>he should read the play through,</u> not paying particular attention to his own part, but in order <u>to find what general impression the play makes upon him,</u> try to discover the author's intention and to imagine himself to be in the audience, seeing and hearing it for the first time. It is very important when reading a play to think of it orally and visually, as if it were in performance. The impression thus formed will, of course, include the actor's own part, but it should appear in its proper relation to the play as a whole.

The actor will then go through the play again, this time reading only the lines of his own part, but reading them aloud to himself. As he does so, a fairly definite picture of the character he is to represent will begin to form in his mind.

He must begin now to soak himself into the part he is to play. He should read carefully not only his own lines but also any lines in the other parts, or stage directions, which may throw light on the character of the person he is to represent. He must try all the time to identify his reading of the part with the author's conception of it. He must feel that he really knows and understands the character as a living person, and can enter into his thoughts and feelings. A poorly written part will offer little reward for such study, and will consequently be difficult to play, for the actor will have to invest it with a personality from his own resources. A well-written part, on the other hand, will provide a wealth of possibilities for interpretation, which the actor will find fascinating to explore.

Trust your Instinct

It is essential that at this stage he should let his instinct guide him rather than his intellect. Acting is very largely instinctive, and if an actor has any talent in him, his theatre-sense will make him feel how the part should be interpreted, and he must have faith in his own imagination. At a later stage it will be necessary for him to corroborate imagination by reason, in order to be able to repeat an interpretation in rehearsal, but that should be definitely a later stage.

There will probably be a certain number of "sticky" passages, where, at a first reading, his actor's instinct fails him entirely, and here he must apply reasoned analysis.

Dangers of being too Subtle

There is a great danger for the intelligent amateur of being over-subtle in interpretation, and consequently theatrically ineffective. One comes across cases of this very frequently.

The actor has arrived at a certain interpretation of a line or speech by a complicated process of psychological reasoning instead of trusting to his actor's instinct—possibly he has little—and he forgets that there is not time for the audience, when they hear the line, to go through a similar process of reasoning. Either they are puzzled and reject the reading, or else they stop to ponder over it, and meanwhile the play has gone on, and they missed what follows.

For instance, the line of Lady Macbeth's in the murder scene:

> ". . . Had he not resembled
> My father as he slept, I had done't . . ."

is sometimes given in a tone weighted with sentimental recollection, instead of being thrown out as a gesture of impatience at her own weakness. Not only is this reading out of character, but it upsets the pace and balance of a scene which is essentially active, and not reflective.

Again, in Shaw's *Fanny's First Play*, there is a scene in which the rather oafish son of the house, Bobby, is seeking instruction in gentlemanly behaviour from Juggins, the footman. He says, "Dora says your name can't be Juggins, and that you have the manners of a gentleman. I always thought you hadn't any manners." The obvious reading of this last line is to stress the word "any", with possibly a slight emphasis on the word "I". One actor playing it put all the emphasis on the word "thought", implying, perhaps, a typically Shavian comment on the manners of gentlemen, but suggesting a witticism of which Bobby would have been incapable, and which would almost certainly fail to get the intended laugh, because it is not in character. It is a mistake always to avoid the obvious. As a rule an audience can grasp a second but not a third curve of a reaction.

Some producers go so far as to say that it is impossible for a person of intelligence to be a good actor, and that the actor must keep his brain in abeyance and follow his instinct, while the producer supplies the intellectual control. There is some truth in this, but it is an over-statement. There is plenty of scope for the intelligent actor, provided that he does not allow his intelligence to swamp his creative impulses.

When the actor has read the play through twice, he will have formed a general idea of the character he is to play, and an outline of the way in which he intends to play it. Detail will come later. He will be wise not to attempt to learn the lines by heart till after he has attended one of two rehearsals. He will find it much easier to memorize his lines when he knows his positions, and in what part of the stage he will be for certain scenes. Moreover, should he once get into his head a wrong interpretation, with which the producer disagrees, he will find it much more difficult to alter it if he has learnt the lines. Producers should insist that lines should be learnt accurately. The actor must respect his author, and give the exact lines the author has written, and no vague substitute of his own "Gagging", even in farce, should be discouraged, except sometimes in an emergency, to cover up some hitch or mistake.

The Actor and the Producer

The actor goes, then, to his first rehearsal with a general idea of the part in his mind, which he is prepared to adapt to that of the producer. The first rehearsal will probably be merely a "walk through" of the whole play, mainly for positions, without attention to interpretation, but from this the actor will be able to form an inkling of the way in which the producer intends to treat the play, and as rehearsals proceed, he will see how his interpretation of his part will fit in with the producer's conception of the play. The producer, on the other hand, will probably be delighted to find that the actor has given some preliminary study to his part, and has brought something of his own to it, and unless the actor's reading of his part is completely irreconcilable with his own scheme for the play, the producer will not want to change it, save in points of detail.

The wise producer realizes that anything the actor has contributed from his own mind is likely to be more effective than something super-imposed upon him from without. In this way there should be perfect co-operation between producer and player. The player must, of course, obey the producer's instruction implicitly; but if the producer asks him to do something for which he cannot understand the reason, he should seek out the producer *after*—not during—rehearsal, and ask him about it. The producer, having thought out the play, ought to be able to give a satisfactory explanation of his instructions, and the player must be prepared to acknowledge this.

On the other hand, the producer must realize that he may be asking the actor to give an interpretation which is incompatible with his particular personality, for the actor must, to a great extent, interpret his part in terms of his own personality. This amount of give and take between actor and producer is essential.

The producer should, of course, never act in his own production, if it can possibly be avoided. It is impossible to concentrate on two jobs at the same time, and both will inevitably suffer.

The Amateur must work Harder

Between rehearsals the actor will return to private study of his part. This is where the amateur usually fails, and where he would do well to imitate the professional. Most amateurs do not work nearly hard enough, either at rehearsal or by themselves. Often, at rehearsal, their interest appears to flag the moment they are not actually wanted on the stage. Instead of watching the producer shaping the play, or gaining experience from the mistakes or successes of their fellow-actors, they will sit at the back of the room, chatting with their friends on other subjects.

Many of them do not give a thought to their part between one rehearsal and the next, save in the matter of learning lines. They leave all the work to be done by the producer. It is sometimes only with difficulty that the producer can persuade his actors to go back and try a passage or scene again. They will say, "Oh yes, I see what you mean," and hurry on to the next speech. Not so the professional. He will take infinite pains to get the exact shade of inflection or timing that the producer requires. He will, of his own accord, go back and take a passage over and over again, and if it still does not satisfy him, he will study it in private.

It would be an excellent thing if amateurs could sometimes watch professionals rehearsing. They would then realize what an enormous amount of detailed and careful work goes into the interpretation of a speech, which probably in performance appears entirely spontaneous and casual. The amateur must work harder if he wishes his public, now grown critical, to take him seriously. He must develop his artistic consciousness until it becomes artistic conscience. He must create for himself a standard of artistic truth, and by that he must judge his own work, not by the plaudits of his public or his local press.

Analyse your own Acting

It is in private study that the actor will begin to translate his imaginative conception of the part more precisely into terms of performance. He will crystallize his ideas, and decide by what means he can obtain the effect he wants to get over to the audience. In rehearsal he will most likely find that what he does bears very little relation to what he intended to do. He will hear his voice giving every inflection but the one he had planned, and so conveying an entirely different significance. Where he had visualized himself moving with ease and grace about the stage, he will feel clumsy and awkward; he will be conscious of lack of control and poise; he will feel the need for technique. He must then bring his analytical mind to bear on his artistic consciousness, and discover, firstly, *what* he is doing wrong; secondly, *why* he is doing it; and thirdly, *how* to put it right. It may take him some time, at first, to develop this critical faculty, but it is absolutely essential, and the only means by which he can hope eventually to give a clear-cut and effective performance. He will find that acting demands intense concentration and energy, but that his imagination and all his faculties are stimulated by responding to that demand, and that his enjoyment will increase with his experience. Every one interested in acting should read Coquelin's essay, *The Art of the Actor*, in which he differentiates very clearly between the dual functions of the actor in his "Number One" (the artist and creator), and his "Number Two" (the critic and technician) capacity.

"Being Natural"

At this point the amateur may argue: "Yes, but in all this cold-blooded analysis and study I shall lose my spontaneity and sincerity. My performance will become entirely artificial." Artificial, yes; insincere, no. All acting is artificial. It is a fine art; almost an exact science. The amateur must rid himself of the idea that he is in any way fulfilling the functions of an actor by simply "being natural". We have suffered long enough from the amateur who feels that all that is required of him is to come on to the stage and behave just as he would in real life. The result, with a few notable exceptions, is entirely ineffective and dull. The function of the actor, like that of any other artist, is not to be natural, nor even to give an imitation of nature, but to give a representation of certain aspects of nature, interpreted in terms of his own personality, and having artistic form and significance. This implies selection; the emphasis of certain features; the suppression of others; and, particularly, the magnifying and projection of those significant aspects in such a way that they assail the consciousness of the audience. Just as the actor makes up his face in order to emphasize his features, so that he may be more clearly seen by the audience, so he must emphasize and enlarge all that he does on the stage.

If, as some "Method" actors do, we behaved on the stage exactly as we should in real life, there would be, for example, a hundred and one little inessential movements, such as scratching the cheek, arranging the hair, fidgeting with clothes or ornaments, hesitation in speech, sniffings, and clearings of the throat, which would immediately irritate and distract an audience. We should carry on an intimate conversation with the people on the stage which would be quite unintelligible and inaudible to any one seated a few yards away. Everything would be perfectly natural, but nothing would stand out clearly, either to eye or to ear. The general effect would be vague, blurred, and monotonous.

It is precisely this indefiniteness and monotony which is the prevailing fault in most amateur acting, and which marks so sharply the distinction between the amateur and the professional. A performance by even a third-rate professional company has at least the merit of clarity of outline, attack, and a certain slickness, which make the story of the play easy to follow, though it may lack the freshness and enthusiasm which often illuminate an amateur performance.

Should the Actor Feel?

Acting must give the appearance or illusion of being natural—if the convention of the play is naturalistic—but in order to do so it must be the result of exact observation and study, controlled by technique. That is acting.

This does not mean that the actor is insincere, uninspired, or unemotional in performance. These qualities are essential parts of his creative (Number One) self, and without them no amount of technique can make his performance interesting. The actor brings his emotional and imaginative faculties most fully into force when he is forming his first conception of the character; he then, in rehearsal, translates it into terms of technique, but, in performance, he re-informs it with a *representation* of that emotion which he experienced when he first studied the part. He uses what Wordsworth would describe as "emotion recollected in tranquillity", intensified by the corroboration of his intellect, and stimulated by the presence of the audience. He is not actually and physically experiencing emotion as he plays, but he is feeling imaginatively, and none the less sincerely, and so his performance, being controlled, and having form, is doubly effective.

That actual emotion has less power to move an audience than simulated emotion has been abundantly proved. For instance, a young amateur actress, highly strung and sensitive, but quite inexperienced, was once playing Juliet. About half-way through the second act she so lost herself in the part that she shed real tears. For the first moment or so the audience was impressed, but presently the tears and sobs increased and could not be checked, the actress became inaudible, her make-up was smeared. Immediately she stepped right out of the play, and the illusion was broken. She ceased to be Juliet, and became merely a young actress who had lost control. The audience were no longer moved, but embarrassed on her behalf.

On the other hand, a well-known professional actress was once rehearsing a scene in which, at a certain cue, she must dissolve into tears. The scene was taken over and over again—perhaps a dozen times in ten minutes—and always, at that cue, the tears (real ones) never failed to well into the actress's eyes and roll pathetically down her cheeks. At the performances the audience was always enraptured, and exclaimed, "Poor thing, how she must feel it! She's really crying". It was a trick admittedly, but one of which the actress had command, and consequently much more effective than the genuine tears of the amateur.

One does occasionally see, in plays acted by quite inexperienced village players or children, an emotional performance which is entirely spontaneous and artless, but which moves us profoundly by the force of its sincerity. Such performances are rare jewels, of which one cherishes the memory, and one would hesitate to impose any kind of technical knowledge on the player for fear he should become self-conscious and lose that sincerity. But the sad thing is that these lovely performances can so seldom be repeated. They have their own value, but it is not that of acting. We are moved more by the personality of the player than by the part he is playing.

The actor must learn to play emotional scenes on technique if he is going to act fairly often, and wishes to increase his experience.

Range and Reserve

It is necessary for the actor to discover the extent of his own emotional range when he is building up his part, so that he knows when to "go all out" and when to play with reserve. This can only be discovered by rehearsal.

He must study the construction of his part, note where its climaxes come, and decide how he can work up to his "big scenes" so that they stand out as high lights in his performance. For instance, supposing that he has a scene early in the play in which he must express anger or annoyance, and, later on, a scene in which he has an outburst of intense fury—as occurs in the part of King Lear, for example—he must not play both these scenes in the same way. If he "goes all out" on the earlier scene, he will have nothing further to give in the later scene. He must keep his force in reserve, if he is to build up to any emotional or tragic climax. This demands practice and experiment.

Producers, therefore, should not have too much patience and sympathy with the player who says that he "cannot feel it" in rehearsal. If he cannot act in cold blood, he is no actor. Nor should the amateur be afraid of getting stale, or fear that his performance will suffer from too much study. No amateur is ever over-rehearsed, and the stimulus of the audience will always give freshness to his performance. There is a world of difference between performance and rehearsal. Performance to different audiences always opens up countless new avenues to explore in a part, even when it has been played every night of the week for several weeks.

The Actor in Rehearsal

We have urged the importance of intensive private study in a part, because it is so often neglected, but the actor's work in rehearsal is equally important. In private, he concentrates chiefly on the interpretation of his own part; in rehearsal, he studies his part in relation to those of the other players. Here he should try to feel himself a part of the producer's pattern, and, above all, he should interest himself in what the other actors are doing.

The plot of a play is like the ball in a game of Rugby football or hockey, which passes continually from one player to another. The producer's job is to see that the attention of the audience is always focused on the ball. The player who holds the ball at the moment is the person whom the audience must watch, and nothing must distract attention from that player. Sometimes the ball will remain with one player for a considerable time as he makes a spectacular dash down the field; sometimes it will pass to and fro between two players; sometimes it will go swiftly to one player after another. All the time the attention of every player is concentrated on the player with the ball, and though the others may not actually be in play themselves, they are not passive; they are alert and poised, ready to receive the ball if it should come their way.

Team-playing

This is the secret of successful team-acting. Each actor can help the story to get over by concentrating his whole mind on it. If he does that, he should never have to ask the producer "What should I do all the time he is speaking? I don't know how to stand or what to do with my hands." The answer is: "Keep still. Watch, and listen to the actor who is speaking. If you are not supposed to be listening, then just keep still."

The actor who is not "in play" should not feel embarrassed or awkward if he remembers that the audience is not looking at him, but at the actor who is speaking, and that it is unnecessary for him to "do" anything, as that would distract attention from the story of the play. At the same time, he must not be a "passenger". It is most important that he should be mentally "in the play". However small his part may be, it is an integral part of the play, and the concentration of his mind upon what is happening

on the stage will greatly help his fellow-actors and the
atmosphere of the scene, while his inattention might completely ruin it. Even though he is not speaking lines, he is
always contributing an important part in the effect of the
scene upon the subconscious mind of the audience.

An illustration of this occurred in a school production
of *Macbeth*. At the moment when Macbeth first sees the
ghost of Banquo, a boy taking the small part of a servant
was in the act of pouring wine into a guest's cup. He had
given himself up so completely to the emotional tension
of the scene that quite unselfconsciously he stopped short
in his action, his eyes following Macbeth's gaze, and
stood, transfixed with horror, staring at the empty chair—
there was no actual visible appearance of the ghost. He
held this position until the ghost vanished, then he relaxed, finished pouring out the wine, and went on with
his business of serving the guests. This piece of sincere
silent acting was of great value to the atmosphere of the
scene, and probably also helped the actor who was playing Macbeth. On the other hand, had the boy overplayed,
and let his reactions be fussy or obtrusive, he would have
destroyed, not enhanced, the illusion.

Study the Other Actors' Lines

The more inexperienced an actor is, the more difficult it
is for him not to be a selfish actor. Nervousness and un-
certainty make it almost impossible for him to think of
anything outside his own part in performance, but consciousness of the other players grows with experience. In
order to help this to develop, the actor, when studying
his part at home, should read aloud the lines of the other
actors with whom he has scenes, particularly where he
has a long scene with only one other actor. Reading the
other people's lines will throw new light on his own part,

and will show him more clearly how to react to their speeches. He may discover that he has been doing something in rehearsal which makes it difficult for another actor to get his effects over, or make his points. It will help him in the timing of his cues and the varying of pace in his own lines. For instance, quite often there is a scene in which one actor, A, has a great deal to say, perhaps a flow of narrative, in which the other's—B's—remarks are only interjections which must be interpolated quickly so as not to check the flow of A's speech. If B has only studied his own lines, he may take up his cues too slowly, or render his relatively unimportant comments with undue emphasis, thereby upsetting the balance of the scene. Actor A, if he were experienced, would soon make things unpleasant for B if he did this, but the amateur is usually too modest, and the producer perhaps not sufficiently knowledgeable, to prevent it.

The listening actor must also remember to appear to be hearing what the other player says for the first time. He must never anticipate an effect or a reaction.

One might mention here in passing the unhelpfulness of inexperienced players when one of them loses his lines. Too often they all stop short and stare in concern at the unfortunate, floundering actor, instead of helping him out by trying to appear as if nothing unusual had happened, in which case the lapse would probably pass unnoticed.

The actor must learn when to efface himself, but also when to "take the stage", and dominate it. Some actors are so modest that it is with the utmost difficulty that the producer can lure them out from behind chairs and tables to take the centre of the stage, or face the audience. If an actor has any stage-sense, he will feel that he must not let himself be masked when he has something important to say, and will unobtrusively clear himself. He will feel, too, when it is necessary to "make an entrance", and not just slink in, clinging to the backcloth, to creep into ambush behind a tall chair. When a whole company is inexperienced, the actor who will help himself in an emergency is a godsend to producers.

The Actor who will be "all right on the Night"

It is quite inexcusable to underplay in rehearsal, particularly when the other actors are novices. The actor who deliberately does this should be expelled from any company without mercy.

One has come across players who will say to the producer, "It's all right, old man, I'm not going all out now. I can't feel it, and I haven't got my lines yet. But don't you worry. It will be all right on the night. You'll be surprised." And we are. The actor will suddenly let loose a flood of emotion, or "funny business", as the case may be, of which he had given no hint at rehearsal, with the result that his fellow-actors, unless they are old hands, will dry up and gape at him, and the producer's pattern for the play will be thrown completely out of balance.

That is the unpardonable crime of the selfish actor.

More often, however, actors underplay in rehearsal from embarrassment and sheer lack of technique. In this again they are not helped by their fellow-actors, who, particularly when love scenes are being rehearsed, are apt to disconcert them by giggling, probably because they, too, feel embarrassed, more than because the scene is being badly played. Many a young actor has been made so self-conscious by the behaviour of those watching rehearsals that he gives up any attempt to play sincerely, with the result that in performance the scene is acted with so little conviction that the audience is inclined to titter. Producers should deal very firmly with anyone who

c

laughs when an actor is trying out a difficult emotional scene. One method is to call upon the mockers to try the scene themselves.

It is very largely on this account that amateurs fight shy of strongly emotional plays and will only commit themselves to something trivial. Emotional scenes must be faced and grappled with in rehearsal, or they are bound to fail in performance. Moreover, if the actor has so rehearsed that he knows that even if he does not feel like it he is certain of getting over at least an adequate effect, he will have greater confidence in approaching the difficult scene.

Finally, the actor should free himself from his script as early as possible after the first two or three rehearsals, particularly if he is a novice. He will never act so long as his eyes are fixed on his book and his hands are encumbered in holding it, nor is it easy for others to act with him. The beginner will tend to cling to his script as long as possible in order to put off the awful moment when he must look up and face his fellow-actors, and, worse, his audience; and when his hands are released to acute consciousness of their existence.

It is perhaps hardly necessary to remind the actor that he must learn his cues—and not just two or three words, but a whole sentence—as well as all cues for entrances or "business".

CHAPTER IV

THE ACTOR'S RANGE OF PARTS

THE actor who wants to learn should bully his producer into letting him attempt many different kinds of parts—tragic, comic, fantastic, romantic, character, or straight—in order that he may acquire range and variety, without which his acting cannot progress. He may find that he is only suited to one type of part, but he cannot be sure of this until he has experimented with many, nor will he have enough range even for one type of part until he has had experience in others. Too many amateurs become "type actors" after one successful performance.

Type-casting

Type-casting in the professional theatre is an acknowledged evil, but it prevails to far too great an extent in the amateur theatre as well, where there is less excuse for it. Both actors and producers are apt to play for safety, and to keep people to parts in which they have previously been successful. Most probably they ultimately defeat their own object, because the inexperienced actor who continues to play the same type of part, without enlarging his general experience, will soon come to the end of his tether, and develop a sameness of style, and probably a host of irritating little tricks and mannerisms, of which his public will begin to tire.

It is good for the serious actor to play comedy sometimes—he will thereby more quickly learn technique—and for the comic actor to attempt serious and emotional parts, and he must remember that he himself is not the best judge of what part suits him. It has been proved repeatedly that, oddly enough, "feeling" one can play a part is no guarantee of success in performance. People very often act better in parts which are uncongenial to them, probably because they are obliged to rely more upon technique.

Juvenile Parts

As a rule the inexperienced actor or actress is least successful in straight juvenile parts, particularly in comedy. A great number of juvenile parts in modern comedies are very thinly written, and depend entirely on the personal charm of the player for their effectiveness.

The young professional actress learns from the first how to exploit her own personality and charm. She is soon made aware of what particular assets she possesses which may attract and please an audience—she probably owes her engagement to them—and she cultivates them for all she is worth. She must. Her career depends upon it. In consequence, her performance has at least a certain individuality and style.

Now the amateur is, as a rule, too "nice" and too modest, as well as too inexperienced, to exploit her own personality. She plays the part quite "straight", behaving just as she would in real life, and relying on the natural charm of youth and good looks to do the rest. Sometimes this is enough, but more often the result is dull. A straight part must have character. The actress must learn to "project" herself. Everything she does must be a little bigger than life-size; the brightness or the wistfulness, the changes from one mood to another, must be clearly defined, even emphasized. The actor must remember that what may appear to him embarrassingly exaggerated as he says or does it on the stage will probably come over to the audience as perfectly natural. The common fault of playing too much "in" to one's fellow-actors, instead of out to the audience, is due very largely to having to rehearse in a small room, where it is very difficult to feel the necessity for this enlarging process.

Projection

It is intensely interesting to be on the stage with experienced professional players; to notice how loud their voices sound; how crisp is their articulation; how controlled is their movement; what a great amount of concentrated energy is behind all that they do; and then to go round in front, and find that it all appears perfectly natural, even casual.

Most amateur playing of juvenile parts is *actually* too casual. The actor is deceived by the apparent ease of just "being himself"; he lacks vigour and attack, as well as variety.

It is really easier, and usually more interesting, for the amateur to play character parts. In a straight part he fits the part on to his own personality; in a character part he must empty his personality into that of the character. He must rely more upon intellect, and less upon histrionic instinct. It is a fascinating business to try to put on an entirely different personality.

Character Parts

To a great extent the character actor builds up his part from observation. As he goes about his daily occupations he is consciously or sub-consciously finding models from everyday life. He will study the characteristics and mannerisms of the people with whom he comes in contact; he will watch people in the street, in trains and buses, in shops, at public gatherings; he will notice the way they walk, the movement of head and hands, how they speak, the sound of their voices, the expression on their faces, both permanent and momentary; he will take this peculiarity from one person and that from another—anything that may help him to give individuality to the character he is to play. Not only will he seek to imitate and reproduce superficial or physical characteristics, but he will try to get inside the minds of his models and understand their thoughts, and the circumstances which make them behave as they do. He will exercise all his sympathy and intuition in this, and with the aid of his own imagination, will build up a complex character that is utterly different from his own. If possible, without being callous, he will also observe people's reaction in emotion—fear, excitement, disappointment, joy, or sorrow, and notice particularly how their voice and movements are affected.

Dangers of Imitation

If he can find all that he wants in one model, so much the better. He should always get his ideas from real life rather than from the stage or cinema, and in particular he should avoid modelling himself on some well-known actor who has played the part. He is only likely to invite unfavourable comparison, and what he has worked out for himself, from his own observation of real life, will be more convincing than a second-hand imitation of someone else. In Shakespearean performances, particularly, there is a great deal of this second-hand acting, which is sometimes slick but seldom sincere, and which robs the play of freshness and life.

One of the reasons why amateurs are wise not to attempt West End successes is that a play which owes its success to the individual performance of some skilled and celebrated actor, for whom it was probably written, is so impregnated with memories of that actor's personality, that it is almost impossible for anyone else playing the part to think of acting it in any other way. Hence we are presented with a rather pathetic array of would-be Margaret Rutherfords, Edith Evanses, and Brian Rixes.

Comedy Parts

The mention of Mr. Rix leads on to the question of the playing of comedy and farce. The amateur still does not appear to have learnt that comedy, especially farcical comedy, is quite the most difficult thing he can attempt. It requires a particularly skilled technique, which can only be acquired by years of constant practice. But as long as audiences continue to applaud the amateur comedian he will, very naturally, continue to play comedy, not realizing that his performance, on its own artistic merits, is not good.

Light comedy parts are difficult because they are all in one key, and within the limits of that key the actor has to find range and variety. The amateur Brian Rix may succeed in being funny for one act, or even an act and a half, but after that he usually becomes tedious, because he has not the mastery of sufficient technical tricks to vary his performance, and his sparkle fails to stay the course.

Then again, pace is essential to farce, and that implies far more time spent on rehearsal than amateurs care to give. Lines must be poured forth with speed and apparent inconsequence, yet comedy-points, as fine as needles, must be made; touched in passing, lightly but definitely. This requires the skill of long experience. Timing is everything. It is said that the late Ralph Lynn had his business so exactly timed that when at one point he lit a cigarette, the match-box had to be placed in a certain position, to an inch, and the match he was to use must be ready sticking out of the box, otherwise his timing would have been upset by several seconds.

The playing of comedy demands considerable command over the audience. The comedian must know how to get a laugh, and how to kill one; when to expect it, and how long to wait for it before resuming; when it is legitimate to hold up the action by "comic business", and when it is not. He must be able to gauge the character of different audiences, and adapt his performance accordingly. A line that "goes hot" with Monday's audience may be stone cold with Tuesday's.

An interesting example of an audience's reactions to comedy points occurred in a revival of *Lady Windermere's Fan*. There is a speech in which the points follow each other in such quick succession that it is impossible for the audience to laugh at each of them. "The Duchess of Berwick", speaking of her husband, says:

"In fact, before the honeymoon was over, I actually caught him winking at my maid—such a pretty, respectable girl. Of course I dismissed her at once without a character. Oh no, I didn't, though. I remember now, I passed her on to my sister-in-law. Her husband, Sir George, is so short-sighted I thought it wouldn't matter (1). But it did, though (2). It was most unfortunate (3)."

A distinguished actress, who was playing the part in her usual richly comic manner, found that she got a big laugh on "I thought it wouldn't matter"; then, by means of skilful timing and pointing, a great roar of laughter on "But it did, though"; but that it was almost impossible to get more than a giggle on "It was most unfortunate". Sometimes she tried to run all three points together in order to get one big laugh at the end, but almost invariably the laugh broke in at point 2 so strongly that she was obliged to wait for it, and "throw away" point 3, the audience having no more breath left to laugh again so soon. Playwrights often make the mistake of packing their comedy points too closely together.

The actor must, moreover, in comedy more than in any other type of play, consider his fellow-actors and play up to them; avoid killing their laughs, or help them to get them; gag, if necessary; "feed" them with a good grace.

Most of the Whitehall farces have been presented by a company that has been playing together for years.

Amateurs should not be discouraged from playing farce, as it is excellent practice in slickness and team-work, but only from being deluded into thinking it is easy.

Most amateur companies should be able to get over a one-act farce successfully, but there are regrettably few really good ones to be found.

Verse Drama

The playing of fantasy or verse drama does not really require a special technique, though it is as difficult to speak verse really well as to sing well, and for most people one demands as much training and practice as the other.

Most of the world's greatest drama is written in verse, and the masterpieces of Æschylus, Shakespeare, Racine, or Eliot, for example, should be approached by the amateur with proper respect and in some trepidation, but it is an essential part of his experience to act in such plays. Great drama begets great acting, and demands vision, strength, and depth in the actor. A diet of West End comedies and "dramas" is no test of real talent, but great verse plays will prove the actor's power and resources to their fullest extent. At the same time, actors and producers should remember that they are dealing with drama

in poetic form, rather than with poetry in dramatic form,
They must not, in the delight of speaking and hearing
beautiful lines, lose sight of the human and dramatic
elements of the play. It is wise to concentrate first on the
drama, and the poetry should inevitably follow, as the
lines live and grow in the actor's memory. If he has any
imagination, ear and sensitiveness to rhythm, the poetic
quality of the play will appear in his speech and throughout his acting. If he has none of these assets, he will be
wise not to attempt verse drama. The responsibility of the
producer for the effectiveness of the play is greater in
verse plays than in any other type.

Illusion and Sustaining a Part

It is only by practice that the amateur can hope to free
himself from the miserable scourge of nervousness which
spoils his performance by blurring the clarity of its
outline.

He must find opportunities of acting more often if he
is to master it. It is all-important that he should succeed
in creating illusion, and his task is not easy. Conditions
are so much against him—a small, ill-equipped stage;
makeshifts and compromises in setting and costume; an
audience that knows him too well. If the audience is to
believe in him, he must be able to sustain his part throughout every moment of the play. How few amateurs ever
succeed in doing this! This is the essential difference, from
the audience's point of view, between amateur and professional acting. In the professional theatre it is easy to be
carried away by the play, and to accept the actors as the
people they are pretending to be. In *The Long, The Short,
and the Tall*, for instance, it was with a shock that one
realized, when the actors took their curtain call, that they
were not, after all, soldiers. This very rarely happens in an

amateur performance, because if the actor slips out of his part for *one moment* he can never get back, as far as the audience is concerned. If he loses a line, and lets the audience see that he has lost it; if he shows himself baffled by some mechanical mishap; if he allows his glance to focus some person in the audience and show recognition—even if he is only a "super" and thinks he is not being noticed—he has stepped right out of the play, and everything that has gone before is of no avail. One slip of this sort from one actor can wreck a whole play. The standard of an amateur performance in which nothing of this sort ever happened would be very high indeed. But it is not impossible; the amateur is not fighting a losing battle with his audience. Conditions of production are improving rapidly, and though the scourge of self-consciousness is still with us, it is not so paralysing as it used to be.

Nervousness

It is consoling to realize that every time the actor plays he gains greater command over his nerves, and also that nervousness in itself is not a bad thing. The most experienced professionals are jagged with nerves on a first night; they would not be good and sensitive actors if they were not. Nervousness, provided that it is controlled, will heighten rather than destroy the value of a performance.

CHAPTER V

TECHNIQUE SELF-TAUGHT

I. SPEECH

MUCH has been said in foregoing chapters about the necessity of acquiring technique, but we hope that the reader has not gained the impression that this is likely to be a very tedious and difficult undertaking. The average amateur can, in a relatively short time, teach himself enough technique to improve the clarity of his performance. As we have tried to show, it is a matter of self-criticism, analysis, and reconstruction.

Audibility

The most important part of the actor's technical equipment is his voice. An inaudible actor is, of course, useless, and sometimes it is impossible to cast an otherwise gifted actor for a part because he is unable to make his voice carry, but this is unusual. Most people can make themselves heard without much difficulty, but they must take trouble about it. Producers, too, must bully their actors in rehearsal, and make sure from the very first that every player is going to be clearly audible in the place in which the play will be performed. If rehearsals are being held in a small hall, the actors should be given an early opportunity of trying the pitch of the hall in which they are to play. The words of the play must come over easily to the audience, for if they have to "work" to hear them, the play stands a poor chance of holding their interest.

The author is indebted to Miss Barbara Storey for suggestions and some of the exercises in this chapter.

A pleasing voice, with a good range of tone, is a great asset to an actor, and some are lucky enough to have this as a natural gift, while others have to labour to acquire it. Quality of voice is all-important in casting a part, perhaps more important than physical appearance. Producers do not always realize this.

Any actor who finds difficulty in being heard would be wise to go to an expert for a course in voice-production. He will find it most helpful. Only the expert who has studied the physical processes of speech can teach him to use his voice rightly. Straining, and other bad habits of speech, are quickly acquired, and difficult to get rid of without such help.

Dangers of the "Beautiful" Voice

In these lessons he should concentrate on the mechanics of voice-production rather than be lured into learning "pieces", dramatic or otherwise, to recite. There is always danger in specialization, and there is grave danger that the actor who makes a special study of elocution may become more concerned with the *manner* than the *matter* of speech. He may be enchanted by the beauty of his own voice, and like to—metaphorically speaking—close his eyes and just sit back and listen to it, fascinated and drugged by the richness of its cadences, but oblivious of the play and the person he is supposed to be in it.

This has been known to happen in the case of actors who have gone in intensively for the speaking of verse, particularly lyrical verse, and rhythmic but undramatic prose.

The effect on an audience is pleasing at first—as music, but not as drama—but later is apt to be soporific.

Again, if the actor "gives recitations" in which he is alone on the platform, and represents all the characters in the piece or play, he becomes so used to having the stage all to himself that it is almost impossible for other actors to play with him. He ignores them, and plays solo and definitely to the audience, thereby stepping out of the play and breaking its illusion. In studying speech, he must always remember that characterization and dramatic values are of the first importance.

Bad habits cling like burrs. One has seen actors striving with all their intelligence to rid themselves of some artificial habit of speech that has been imposed on them, but which has become so much a part of them that they cannot cast it off.

Some years ago there was much unintelligent teaching of voice-production and elocution, and teachers built up an entirely wrong technique, which, being superficial, fostered insincerity. We still see products of this method, whose articulation is oppressively painstaking, and whose acting will always appear forced and artificial.

Nowadays, however, there are so many excellent teachers of the subject that the amateur should find little difficulty in obtaining the help of a qualified expert from some such recognized school as the Central School of Speech Training, or the Rose Bruford College. There are, moreover, many excellent textbooks on the subject, such as Gwynneth Thurburn's *Voice and Speech*, which the actor can study for himself. No attempt will be made here to deal with the physical technicalities of voice-production.

Most of the common faults in speech are due either to lack of breath-control, lack of ear, or lack of speech-energy.

Breath-control

Under "Lack of Breath-control" the following faults may be classified:

1. *Inaudibility.*—Failure to make the voice carry, owing to an insufficient volume of tone controlled by an adequate supply of breath.

2. *Fading away of Voice* at the end of a sentence. The uneven, gusty effect evident in so many performances, when the actor's voice dies away to nothing, is due to his not having sufficient breath in reserve to last out the sentence.

3. *Speaking too rapidly.*—Very often due to nervousness. The actor feels his tone giving out, and hurries to fit in his words before it does.

4. *Hoarse or Tired Voice* at the end of a play, due to forcing the voice out by muscular tension in the throat and upper chest. Such tension impedes the free flow of breath to the resonators, and thereby affects tone. It also strains the larynx, and has a bad effect on the vocal cords themselves.

Elementary Breathing

EXERCISE 1.

Silent—Place your hands just above your waistline, with the tips of the middle fingers touching each other. Take a deep breath through the nose, taking care not to stiffen or tighten the neck, chest, or shoulders, and feel your hands being pushed forwards and outwards, and the finger-tips gradually drawing away from each other. On no account must the hands be drawn downwards and inwards.

EXERCISE 2

Voiced—Holding the hands in the same position, take a deep breath in the same way and let it out on a prolonged hum on "m". Vibration should be felt on the inner edge of the lips and in the front of the face. Repeat with the syllable "mah", holding the "m" for an appreciable time before passing to the vowel. The "ah" should sound as clear and free from "breathiness" as the "m", and should be projected to the front of the face". Finally, drop the "m" and use "ah" only, avoiding any suggestion of throatiness.

It is a good thing to practise such exercises daily, particularly just before a rehearsal, and a few deep breaths taken in the way described help greatly in steadying the voice and nerves before going on the stage for a performance.

Ear-training

The faults due to lack of Ear are mainly:

A. *Monotony* in tone and pace. This is the worst and the most common defect in amateur acting. More than anything, the actor should cultivate the effective use of Range, Variety, and Contrast in his speech. The speaking voice has a possible range of at least two octaves, and the actor must have a conscious control over his full range. Monotony in speaking is due not so much to using a small range, but to using the *same* range over and over again. The normal conversational range is about an octave, and it is used, unconsciously, by every speaker. This unconscious speech habit must be controlled, and smaller and therefore more varied ranges of pitch must be used. The actor must train his ear to listen to his own voice, hear what it is doing, and make it do what he wants. If he finds it difficult to hear what his voice is doing, and impossible to control it, he should study intonation under the guidance of a skilled teacher, preferably a phonetician.

B. *Catching the Tone of the Other Players* so that every one

in the scene plays on the same note. The actor must listen
to the tune, not only of his own voice, but of the play as a
whole. The same applies to rhythm and pace.

C. *Wrong Emphasis.*—Stressing the unimportant words,
or failing to stress the important words in a sentence.
This is also a very prevalent fault, and apparently very
difficult to cure. At first it must seem that it is due to unintelligent reading of the part, but it has frequently been
proved that an actor can understand the meaning of what
he is saying, and yet fail completely to convey that meaning, by stressing wrong words, particularly if he is speaking in an idiom, and using turns of phrase which are unfamiliar to him. Often he seems unable to hear which
word he is emphasizing. For example, this occurred in the
rehearsal of a certain scene. The girl asks:

"Why are you so sulky, Simon?"

Simon replies:

"I'm not sulky."

The actor said the line with all the emphasis on the
word "I". The producer asked him to say the line with all
the stress on the word "not", and repeated it for him in
that way. The actor then said the line with the emphasis
again on the "I", exactly as before, and though he tried
the line over and over again, he was apparently quite incapable of hearing the difference.

The same thing happens with inflections. Often people
seem unable to hear the difference between an upward
and a downward inflection, either in their own voice or
other people's.

D. *Wrong Pronunciation*, particularly of vowel sounds.
An actor with a good ear will probably be able to reproduce any kind of vowel sound, and therefore any type of
speech or dialect. His aim should be to rid himself of
dialect or accent when necessary, or to assume it; he

D

ought, for instance, to be able to speak in broken English, differentiating between a French, German, or Italian accent, and an American or Scottish accent, provided that he has a model to listen to. He ought to be able to imitate not only the characteristic vowel sounds, but the inflections and general tune of the speech, when he has heard it spoken for a considerable time, so that he has got the sound of it thoroughly into his head. For this purpose the dialect records issued by the British Drama League, 9 Fitzroy Square, London, W.1, are invaluable.

Dialect and Standard English

Pure dialect is a heritage of which we are rightly proud, and which we are anxious to preserve. As a rule, the broader and dipthongized vowels of dialect speech are richer in tone and more pleasing to listen to than those of Standard English. It is a pity to try to make natural dialect speakers use Standard English when they act, as the result will probably be a self-conscious and stilted parody of it. So long as there is a measure of uniformity in the speech of the players, and their articulation is sufficiently distinct —which, unfortunately, it very often is not, in dialect speaking—it is preferable that they should speak in the language natural to them.

Less pleasing and equally difficult to alter are the modified or debased forms of dialect which are much spoken by town-dwellers—a kind of hybrid speech, part dialect and part Standard English, in which the broad dialect vowel sounds have become flattened and weakened into something singularly unattractive. In this case it is advisable to encourage the player to cultivate his ear until he has mastered the sounds of Standard English.

Ear-training

The following are useful exercises for practising variety of tone and pitch:

EXERCISE 3

Control—Take a deep breath, and count aloud slowly from 1 to 8, speaking each number on a tone higher than the last, being careful to speak and not sing the notes. There are, moreover, eight different vowel sounds in the eight numbers. Ask somone to listen to you and tell you whether you are really getting a distinctly different note on each word.

EXERCISE 4

Range—A similar effect can be practised by saying the nursery rhyme, "Mary, Mary, quite contrary," on an ascending speaking scale, reaching the highest note on the word "silver", and thence descending to the lowest note on the word "row".

Be careful, in each case, to start on as low a note as you can, without straining, otherwise your highest note is likely to become a squeak. Most people, women particularly, would do well to develop the low and lower-middle tones of their voice. As a rule, the voice carries best on the middle and upper-middle notes, but if only these are used the effect is monotonous. In plays acted by all-women casts, the general effect of the speech is one of uniform thinness and shrillness of tone, and the ear longs for the contrast of a man's voice, or for someone to break the monotony by striking a lower and richer tone, which would give body, strength, and variety to the voice-pattern of the play.

Lack of Speech-Energy

In addition to the faults caused by lack of ear and breath-control, there is the all-pervading weakness of slovenly speech, which seems to be characteristic of our generation, and which is due solely to laziness and lack of effort in the forming of words. It is the product of the listlessness prevalent since the war. It is not difficult to cure, provided that people can be persuaded that such a habit of speech is a liability and not an asset.

The "Contemporary" Voice

People do not bother to move their lips or part their teeth when speaking, and often use very little speechenergy. The result is that consonants are barely articulated, and vowel sounds become flattened almost out of recognition—most particularly the long "o" sound—the same indeterminate quality doing duty for them all. Our English vowel sounds, though perhaps not so pleasing as those of other languages, are not without beauty when given their true value.* This disregard of vowel sounds is one of the most striking and one of the ugliest features of modern speech. Our whole manner of speech is anæmic and feeble, lacking in vigour and clarity. This is probably the main reason why our younger actors and actresses so frequently fail in the playing of Shakespeare, and other verse or "classical" plays. They are unable to rid themselves of that manner of speech which stamps them so unmistakably as "Contemporary".

If one observes people in ordinary conversation, and often also on the stage, one notices that very rarely is any space visible between the two rows of teeth as they speak. Frequently their lips hardly appear to move at all, and not

---

* Often we are faced with such grim alternatives as the following (quoted, I think, by Mr. George Sampson):

East End congregation: "Prise 'im for 'is grice and fiver."

West End congregation: "Preese Him for His greece and fever."

even the teeth are visible. It is a good thing to practise speaking while looking in a mirror in order to see whether one is really opening one's mouth. In the formation of the open vowel sounds there should be at least half an inch of black space visible between the upper and lower teeth. A great many people speak the rounded vowel sounds "o", "oo", "aw" with their mouths in the same position as for the sound "ee", hence the flattening of what should be full, rounded sounds. Any good textbook on diction gives exercises in the formation of vowel sounds, which should be seriously practised. The following lines are useful for this purpose:

1. "O spectres busy in a cold, cold gloom!
    O lank-eared phantoms of black-weeded pools!
    Why do I know ye? Why have I seen ye?"

2. "Blue thistles bloomed in cities; foodless toads
    Within voluptuous chambers, panting, crawled."

3. ". . . How still the evening is,
    As hush'd on purpose to grace harmony!"

4. "Life is a pure flame, and we live by an invisible sun within us. A small fire sufficeth for life; great flames seemed too little after death, while men vainly affected funeral pyres, and to burn like Sardanapalus."

The Open Throat

In order to produce bright, clear tone, not only must there be good direction of the breath and adequate flexible jaw movement, but the throat must be "open". A good exercise for increasing the capacity to open the throat is to yawn, feeling the soft palate rise and the back of the tongue depress itself. Then repeat the yawn with

with the lips closed. In making vowel sounds, the tip of the tongue should rest against the bottom teeth. This checks the tendency to retract the tongue and thus block the free passage of breath fom the throat into the mouth.

Over-careful Articulation

While most people should make more effort in articulation than they normally do, exaggeratedly careful and conscious articulation and pronunciation are faults in the opposite direction, equally tiresome. This is particularly evident in the too-careful utterance of unimportant words and syllables, such as "and", or the prepositions "to" and "for"; the monotonous emphasis on the pronoun "I"; the "ed" termination of verbs, and the middle syllable of such a word as "interested". The careful separation of final and initial dental consonants in words such as "told to", "what did", is usually unnecessary. The first of the two consonants should be firmly articulated, and held for the length of time occupied by both consonants. The attack on the second consonant is felt as an added impulse of energy, strengthening, but not altering, the articulation. Unless this added length and energy are felt by the speaker, he is in danger of leaving one of the consonants out altogether, which is just as bad a fault as exaggeration of them. If the mind is concentrating on the meaning and rhythm of the words spoken, these elaborations of manner should not occur.

While over-careful articulation is a fault to be avoided, consonant sounds must be given due attention. They are, to human speech, what the skeleton is to the human body. Vowels may carry more of the tone-quality of voice, but consonants carry vigour. If speakers rely on vowel sounds to carry their voice as well as to give variety of tone, they will find that the volume of tone necessary to make themselves heard will be so great that *variety* of tone becomes almost impossible.

Vigorous, well-articulated consonants give distinctness and "drive" to the spoken word, and are capable of carrying any weight of tone. Apart from this fundamental power of consonants, the fact that it is possible to lengthen and strengthen them, for purposes of emphasis, gives them a great "emotional" value. Again, a vigorous, well-controlled articulation means a good attack and a clean finish in phrasing—a most important matter.

While it is essential for the actor to practise speech exercises daily, he should not use the lines for a part he is rehearsing as exercises in such purely mechanical things as breathing, pitch, and articulation, or a certain stilted artificiality may creep into his reading of the part and damage its sincerity. He should take exercises from text books, and then, with his technique absorbed into his subconscious mind, practise the speeches in his part, concentrating entirely on the meaning and value of the lines, deciding how best to express them, by means of emphasis, rhythm, balance, and contrast in tone and pace.

The actor must remember that the audience must get the impression that the words the actor says are being spoken and thought for the first time. It is fatal to illusion if it is apparent that they are lines learnt by heart.

Variety in Long Speeches

It is not easy for the actor, who has rehearsed the play so often, to appear as if he had no idea of what was coming next. He is apt to anticipate an effect quite unconsciously, but it is fatal. Amateurs frequently fail in this way, particularly in their longer speeches, which they tend to rattle off at a uniform pace, without pauses, and all on one note. Actors should study their long speeches very carefully, noticing which are the most important sentences in each speech, and which are the most important words in each sentence, and deciding how the speech as a whole can be broken up and varied.

Broadly speaking, every change of idea should imply a change in tone and pace, and should usually be marked by a pause. An important sentence can be made to stand out from the others by a pause before and after it. The following speech from Susan Glaspell's *Trifles* affords a good example of this:

"She, come to think of it, was kind of like a bird herself —real sweet and pretty, but kind of timid and fluttery. How she did change. . . . Tell you what, Mrs. Peters, why don't you take the quilt in with you? It might occupy her mind."

The person referred to in this speech is a neighbour living on a lonely farm, who has been arrested on suspicion of having murdered her husband. The climax of the speech is the sentence, "How she did change". The preceding sentence would probably be spoken in a lighter tone, as the sound of the words suggests, with a touch of reminiscent pathos. Then there would be a pause, and on the climax-line the voice would drop to a lower and heavier tone, and the pace would be slower, in order to give a suggestion of something grim and rather sinister. After the pause at the end of this sentence the voice would completely change again, as the idea changes to something practical,. The tone would be stronger and crisper, and the pace would be taken up much more quickly.

An abrupt change in tone and pace always arrests the attention of an audience. Here is a good exercise for practice in this:

"I went up to Mary's room; the door was locked—and there was a thin stream of blood oozing out from under the door."

The first half of the sentence should be spoken rapidly and on a high note, and should be broken off sharply after the word "locked". After a pause of about two seconds, the voice should drop to as low a note as possible, and the rest of the sentence should be taken slowly and softly.

Sometimes the pauses which are to "frame" an important sentence are almost imperceptible, as in this speech from *Hamlet*:

"I say we will have no more marriages: those that are married already, all but one, shall live: the rest shall keep as they are."

The words "all but one" should be made to stand out by means of a tiny pause, before and after them, rather than by an increase in emphasis or volume. Joan's speech from the trial scene (*St. Joan* Scene vi.) beginning: "Yes, they told me you were fools," is excellent for practice in breaking up a long speech and building it gradually up to a climax. The whole speech is intensely emotional, and yet the decorative and poetic quality of the descriptive passages must be given their full value. Here, as in the extract from *Trifles*, the sound echoes the sense of the words, and the tone of the voice will change with each new thought. All this, however, must not break the emotional unity of the speech, nor prevent its pace and rhythm from sweeping up to the great final climax, "I know that your counsel is of the devil, and mine is of God."

The following exercise has been found very useful for general practice, as in it are combined all the points we have dealt with—breathing, range, pitch, tone, articulation, vowel and consonant values, attack, rhythm, and pace:

"Hark to the trump and the drum!
 And the mournful sound of the barbarous horn,
 And the flap of the banners that flit as they're borne,
 And the neigh of the steed, and the multitude's hum,
 And the clash, and the shout, They come! They come!"

Each line should be taken on one speaking note, starting as low as possible, and at first on one long breath and with the last word of each line sustained for two beats. The tone should flow evenly through the line and not be allowed to become staccato. Then at a later stage, the breath should be adjusted to the varying length of the phrases. Long-sustained breathing is not the only kind of breathing necessary, and it tends to produce smooth, flowing tone at the expense of vigour and variety of tone, and also to destroy the phrase pattern.

As the pitch of the voice rises a tone on each line, so the volume and pace correspondingly increase, so that the verse which begins almost in a whisper, low but tense, ends on a high, but not shrill, shout.

Speaking generally, the three important things the actor must always remember about speech are TO THINK, TO LISTEN, TO MOVE HIS MOUTH.

CHAPTER VI

TECHNIQUE SELF-TAUGHT

II. MOVEMENT

JUST as in Speech the fundamental principles to be mastered are control of the breath and training of the ear, so the secret of good movement on the stage lies in control of the weight in the body, and the cultivation of a sense of poise and form.

It would appear that only those few people who have an instinctive stage-sense have any feeling for movement on the stage. The majority of people move clumsily and awkwardly, and appear to be quite unconscious of what their bodies are doing. On the whole, women are worse in this respect than men; they seem to have less sense of poise, and less control of their movements.

Once an actor has become aware of what his body is doing, and what it will look like to the audience, the battle is half won. It only remains for him to make his body do what he wants, and for that process to become subconscious.

In order to acquire poise and control, it is of great value to attend classes in gymnastics, fencing, Greek dancing, movement, and dance drama, particularly of the type taught by exponents of Modern Dance. In making a special study of mime, just as in specializing in elocution, there is a slight danger of introducing too much gesture into a spoken play, and the actor must guard against this temptation.

Only the underlying principles of movement can be taught, and gesture, as a separate thing, cannot be taught at all. All movement and gesture in acting must be the spontaneous and vital expression of some impulse from within, otherwise it is meaningless and ineffective. No actor should ever make a movement or gesture unless he knows exactly what he means by it, and unless it is necessary, either to the action of the play—which is the producer's business—or to express or emphasize an idea or emotion which dould not be expressed without it. All movements must be clear-cut, rhythmic, significant, and, to a certain extent, decorative. In most amateur acting there is too much restless and fidgety movement, and a great deal of unnecessary, artificial, and inexpressive gesture.

This is due partly to nervousness,and one of the first things the actor must learn is to relax, stand still, and to keep still, if necessary, for minutes on end (see page 24). In order to do this, he must learn to feel how his weight is distributed.

Elementary Exercises in Weight-Control

EXERCISE 5

Standing Still. Just as it is helpful to take several deep breaths before going on the stage to play a part, so it is good to "collect" one's weight before going on. Stand for a few moments with your feet together, and feel that your weight rests evenly on the balls—*not* the heels—of both feet, and that it is thrown slightly forward, the knees braced, but not stiff, the shoulders back, and the head up, but relaxed, while the arms hang loosely and comfortably; the hands, when allowed to fall naturally, will come forward a little. Get your balance by rising once or twice on your toes. You will then feel that your weight is under control, and poised, and that you are ready to move smoothly and easily in any direction.

Try also, as an exercise in poise, standing still in the

position described, making sure that you feel comfortable and easy in it; then hold the position, keeping perfectly still without fidgeting for twenty seconds.

From this, go on to a further exercise in weight-control.

Walk fairly briskly round the room, stopping short every now and then, with the entire weight of your body resting on the front foot, the front knee braced, the back leg quite relaxed. Make sure that all your weight is supported by the front leg, by raising the foot of the relaxed leg from the floor, without wobbling. Do this several times, until you can be certain of coming easily to a stand-still in your walk, without the slightest over-balancing. Then try stopping with the weight all thrown on to the back foot, when you will find the weight must fall on the heel. This is not so easy nor so graceful. You will feel that as you swing over your weight on to the back leg, you want to turn your body slightly to the side from the hips, otherwise your position will be uncomfortable and awkward.

Practise standing with one leg advanced, and, without moving the position of your feet, transfer your weight from the front leg to the back, and vice versa, first quickly, then slowly.

Exercise 6

Elementary Stage Moves and Crosses. Once you have learnt to feel how your weight is distributed, you are ready to try short walks across the stage.

Start from the upper right-hand corner of the stage to cross to a chair down left. First collect your weight, and then, as it were, "aim" it at the place you are going to. Project your weight forward, and let your body follow its direction. This does not mean that you must fix your gaze upon the chair to which you are going. It is purely a mental and imaginative process.

EXERCISE 7

Sitting and Rising. When you reach the chair, stop in front of it, and close enough to feel that the back of the calf of one leg is touching it. (Never look round to make sure it is there!) Then, as you sit down, transfer all your weight on to one leg, and you will find you are sitting in a comfortable and sufficiently graceful position, with your knees and feet close together, and with one foot slightly advanced. When you rise, push off with the weight on the back foot, and, as your knees straighten, transfer it entirely to the front foot. You are then ready to move away in any direction. Practise this until you can do it smoothly and easily.

Let us make it clear at this point that this is *not* to be taken as a Rule for the Only Right Way of Sitting Down. Here again, there are no rules; and there are, of course, a hundred different ways of crossing a stage and sitting down, varying according to the character and situation in the play.

In movements of action or aggression, such as anger, eagerness, delight, expectation, or supplication, the weight tends to be thrown forward; while in movements of reaction or defence, such as fear, disappointment, or refusal, it is drawn backwards. It is certainly much easier to play an intimate or emotional scene with a person if both players have their weight thrown towards each other, particularly in love scenes and stage embraces. When these look clumsy, it is almost invariably because the actors have got their weight on the wrong feet. If the girl has her weight on the foot farthest away from the man, it is impossible for him to hold her in a graceful position. In this connection there is a useful axiom that "Power comes from the right". It is much easier to play a strong scene from the left of the stage, with the left cheek in profile, and the right foot advanced, and the right hand nearest the person addressed. Producers would do well to bear this in mind when working out the movements for their actors, and should arrange their grouping so that the principal person in the scene may have his left profile to the audience.

Direction in Movement

We have said that all movement on the stage should be clear-cut, definite, and rhythmic. The actor will find it a help, when practising his part, to mark out his movements first in a diagram in his book, and then on the floor of the stage or room in which he rehearses. This will enable him to time his movements accurately. If, for instance, he has a long speech—perhaps a soliloquy—during which he paces up and down, each turn and crossing of the stage should be timed to a definite cue, and should be marked out by lines on the stage. However short a distance he has to go, the actor should cultivate the feeling of going from one definite spot to another, in a certain rhythm. For example, the producer tells an actor to "go over to So-and-so." The inexperienced actor will shuffle a few in-definite steps *in the direction* of So-and-so, but fail to reach him by several feet, instead of walking smoothly and definitely right up to the person and stopping there. Amateurs appear to have the greatest reluctance to going really close to their fellow-actors. They should remember that it is very difficult to play any tense or emotional scene with a person at arm's length. It is often effective in a love scene or a quarrel scene to see two people with their faces almost touching.

"Backing"

Another habit of the novice, which weakens his stage crosses, is to move to the spot required and then retreat *backwards* from it to the place from which he started. This happens surprisingly often, and it is difficult to find the psychological reason for it. Sometimes it is because the actor becomes panic-stricken at finding himself in a more conspicuous position on the stage, and feels he must retire surreptitiously to a comparatively secluded spot, but more often, if the producer stops the actor and asks him why he is backing, he will reply, "Oh, was I? I never noticed." This shows his lack of body-consciousness and control.

Movement on a Small Stage

Even if the stage is so small that there is only a distance of about six feet to be covered, the actor must so move, with purpose and direction, that, while taking small steps, he gives the impression that a significant movement is being made, smoothly and easily, even though he could actually cover the distance in a couple of lurching strides. The actor has to cultivate a sense of scale and proportion in his movements. As we said in Chapter III., it is not effective to move on the stage just as we should in real life. It is something of an achievement to be able to move about a small stage, heavily encumbered with furniture, in such a way as to create an illusion of space and freedom. Unfortunately, many inexperienced producers arrange their stage furniture much as they would set a course for an obstacle race. In this connection the question of *turning* on the stage always appears to baffle the amateur, even when he is not encumbered with furniture. Almost invariably it looks better and easier to the audience if the actor turns towards them, rather than away from them, when crossing the stage or making an exit. Thus, if the actor is in the centre of the stage, facing front, and he is to go out at the left upper entrance, he should turn to his *left*, which is the shortest way. If he turns to the right he has, of course, farther to go to reach the exit, and the movement looks clumsy. Even if the actor is standing in profile, with his left side to the audience, he should still turn to his left if he is to exit on the left. This would seem obvious, but it is astonishing how seldom amateurs seem to realize it. One sees that awkward threequarter turn over and over again.

Once the actor has begun to gain control of his weight, he should try to develop a sense of line with regard to his own body, and also with regard to his own body in relation to the bodies of the other players on the stage. The actor should be conscious of the decorative possibilities of his body, at rest, or in motion. He should think of its line, from his head to his heels, remembering how it will look to the audience, and that the curve of the spine is its most significant part. Sometimes an actor breaks the rhythmic curve of his body by keeping his head at a wrong angle, and not letting it complete the curve of the spine, or he may break it by ugly angles of the hip, knee, or foot. In diagram A, of a figure in profile, kneeling, there are five different angles; in B there are only two. It is usually more effective to kneel on the knee nearest to the audience. (See illustration p. 60.)

Note, too, the difference made in the curve of the body by the position of the head in diagrams C and D, which represent a figure drooping in dejection or fatigue.

The actor cannot, as a rule, see what his body is doing, but he can form a mental picture, and should be able to *feel* when he is in a certain pose.

He should cultivate range and variety in his movement,

E

The angle of the head in relation to the
curve of the spine.

just as in his voice, and also in his static poses. He should recognize the varying values of playing in profile, full face, threequarter face, and with his back to the audience. It is very often effective to stand with one's back to the audience—a great deal can be expressed by an actor's back—and then turn the head to the side, so that part of one cheek only is revealed to the audience. The white triangular portion of the face, framed by the back of the head and the shoulder, which are dark, has value by contrast. (See illustration below.)

Varying positions of the head when playing with back to the
audience.

Some actors, partly from self-consciousness, tend to play too much in profile. Producers should be on the look-out for this, and make the actor vary his positions, and play facing front when necessary. It is irritating to the audience never to see the whole of a player's face, or to get the full value of his expression.

The Effect of Emotion on Movement

The actor's movements must, of course, vary with the part he plays, both in character and in mood. It is useful to realize that the difference in the effect of various emotions upon movement is largely a question of whether the body is tense or relaxed. Here, again, some people seem to find great difficulty in feeling the difference between a tense and a relaxed movement.

EXERCISE 8

Relaxation—A helpful exercise for this is to walk a few steps and pause, with the weight on the front foot; then gradually raise the arms, with the hands and fingers stretched forwards and upwards, bending the head slightly backward, until the whole body is stretched tense, reaching upwards. The fingers, particularly, must finish the movement (Fig. E). When that position has been held

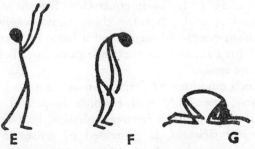

Exercise in tense and relaxed movement.

for a moment, all the muscles of the body should be relaxed; the neck, elbows, shoulders, and knees should give slightly; then the arms should be gradually lowered, drawn down from the elbows; while the head and the whole body bend (Fig. F), and very slowly sink into a kneeling and, finally, a crouching position, with the forehead touching the ground (Fig. G). Then reach up again into the tense position, hold it, and down again to the relaxed position. The repetition of these movements is excellent for suppleness.

Strong emotions, such as fear, anger, love, desire, hate, joy, tend to make the body become tense. It is almost impossible to play a strong quarrel or love scene without instinctively contracting all the muscles of the body, neck, shoulders, legs, and, above all, hands and fingers. Such a scene will entirely fail to convince if the actor allows his fingers to hang loose and inert.

The contracting of the neck and throat muscles tends to constrict the tone of the voice and make it harsh, which helps the effect of strong emotion in an exclamation or short sentence, but if the actor has a speech of any length to say he must relax these muscles or he will force and strain his voice. He can still get his effect by keeping the other muscles of his body contracted. Breathing, too, is important. A visibly heaving chest always heightens the effect of an emotional scene, and it helps in "getting up steam" for a scene if the chest begins to work before any words are spoken.

In such emotions as despair, disappointment, shame, weariness, the body will become limp and relaxed. Similarly, the contrast between physical heat and cold, health and sickness, is expressed by tense or relaxed movement.

It may seem unnecessary to emphasize the need for the physical expression of emotion, but acting, which is good in other respects, has so often been known to miss its effect by its failure to co-ordinate mind and body, and even sometimes because the movements of the actor's body are a contradiction of the words he is saying.

EXERCISE 9

(For two people)

The following is an emotional variation on the exercises on pages 54 and 55.

Two people start walking across the room towards each other; after a few steps they stop short in surprise at seeing each other. After the pause of amazement, continue the meeting, registering (*a*) delight, (*b*) anger, (*c*) fear, (*d*) embarrassment.

The Effect of Character on Movement.
Old Parts

Again, movement must be modified to express the character which is being impersonated. So far, we have been thinking in terms of straight parts, where the weight is assumed to be under proper control. In playing parts of old, sick, tired, or clownish people, the movements will be entirely different, because the weight is not under control. An old or infirm person is not able to shift his weight easily from one leg to another. He will tend to support his weight evenly on both feet, and on the heels rather than the balls. His movements will be slow and hesitant, his step without spring. He will not sit down or rise in one easy, graceful movement, but in two or three angular, difficult stages, seeking extra support for his weight on the arms of the chair, or a stick. His head movements, particularly, will be slower. The eyes will move first, and the head follow the direction of the eyes. His hand movements will be stiff and fumbling, and on the whole he will move much less than a young person. Stillness very much helps the effect of old age, far more so than the palsied shakings and mowings so often affected by stage "gaffers". Moreover, it is easier for a young person to suggest age by means of movement than by means of make-up.

Timid or delicate people may move with head and knees slightly bent, walk with short steps, their feet in a straight line; sit on the edge of their chair, feet, knees, and hands pressed together; fidget, blink, constantly shift their gaze: while strong, confident people will move with a firm, easy step; sit or stand with feet well apart, head up, eyes steady.

The Effect of Period on Movement

Period also affects movement, though this is largely a question of costume. An actor with any stage-sense will instinctively adapt his movements to his costume the moment he puts it on. The character of the costume will suggest freedom or restriction of movement; naturalness or artificiality. It is essential, however, for actors to be given practice in the wearing of period costumes, long before the dress rehearsal, particularly when cloaks, trains, crinolines, armour or swords have to be manipulated.

Exercise 10

Cross the stage and sit down (a) as yourself; (b) eagerly; (c) timidly; (d) languidly; (e) as if you had received bad news; (f) thoughtfully.

Notice and analyse the difference in your positions.

EXERCISE 11

Cross, and sit in an armchair as (*a*) an old and rheumatic person; (*b*) a sick or exhausted person; (*c*) a stout countryman or woman; (*d*) a medieval prince or princess; (*e*) an Early Victorian lady or gentleman.

EXERCISE 12

(For two people)

Take up what you think would be an effective pose for a proposal scene in (*a*) 1460; (*b*) 1760; (*c*) 1860; (*d*) 1960, bearing in mind the decorative value of the outline of both bodies in relation to each other.

Lyn Oxenford's *Playing Period Plays* (Garnet Miller) is helpful on this subject.

Gesture

As we said above, gesture cannot be separated from movement; it is a detailed part of it, if by gesture we mean mainly the movements of hands and arms. It is simply a question of degree. However slight a gesture is, it is none the less a movement, expressing an idea or emotion, and the whole of the body is concerned in it, even though only the hand or fingers may be seen to move.

For example, the emotion of fear might be expressed by a crouching movement of the whole body, with the arm flung up, shielding the head, the palm of the hand turned outwards, fingers outstretched, every muscle taut, and the eyes staring; or it might be expressed by just a barely perceptible movement of the hands—a momentary clenching of the fingers, a drawing back of the elbows, with a sharp intake of the breath, and a quick glance of the eyes; but if the actor is *feeling* fear with his imagination, his whole body will be none the less tense, though the contracting of the muscles is hardly visible to the audience.

The face—especially the eyes—and the fingers are the most mobile and the most expressive parts of the body, and the actor ought to be able to convey all he wants by these alone.

The eyes are all-important, and if the actor is really feeling his part, his eyes are bound to be expressive. Sometimes, however, the novice is so overcome with embarrassment that he will keep his eyes fixed on the ground, and can only with the utmost difficulty be persuaded to cast an occasional fleeting glance at his fellow-actors, or out in the direction of the audience. The producer should accustom him to meeting the gaze of the other actors at an early stage in rehearsals. The direction of the eyes is an indication of the actor's thoughts, and when he is thinking about someone on the stage his eyes should be focused on that person. When he is thinking more subjectively, he will probably look into space, preferably in the direction of the audience, but he should never look *at* them, but fix his gaze on a point just above their heads. On no account should he look, or seem to look, at a particular person in the audience.

The type and degree of gesture will depend very largely on the convention and period in which the play is written, and the style of the production.

All hand movements, however slight, should be made freely and easily from the shoulder and not from the elbow. The position of the hand, and the character of the gesture, if controlled by the mind of the actor, will be appropriate to the idea he wishes to express; if not, they will be valueless.

It is useless for a producer to say to an actor, "Now you might stretch out your arms towards her." The actor will obediently raise his arms, and hold them out in the direction indicated, with the hands and fingers either stretched stiffly out, or hanging limply, the fingers curled and lifeless.

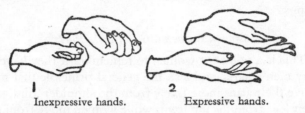

1   Inexpressive hands.   2   Expressive hands.

Unless the actor can feel that a gesture suggested to him is helping him in what he wants to express, he should never make it. Super-imposed gestures only look artificial and unconvincing, as also do consciously graceful, "pretty" gestures.

There was a time when every amateur leading lady, whenever she spoke a line, would raise her hands, fingers curved gracefully upwards, and stand exactly like a wax-work mannequin in a draper's window. Interesting relics of this school of thought are still occasionally to be found. The movement was vaguely graceful and coy, but quite meaningless, and was due, probably, to a self-conscious inability to stand still.

It is rather more difficult for a woman to stand well on the stage than for a man. A man can stand erect with his hands at his sides, without looking unduly stiff, and there are many ways in which he can dispose of his hands. In modern dress he can put them in trousers or jacket pockets; he may fold his arms, clasp his hands behind him, or sometimes put them on his hips. In period costume he still has a belt or sword hilt on which to rest his hands. Nearly all these positions are considered ungainly for a woman in a straight part, and there is little choice between letting them hang at her sides and clasping them in front of her. Hence her frequent resort to handkerchiefs, handbags, cigarettes, or chains of beads to toy with. But she must teach her hands to be at ease without touching things.

Women's movements in Men's Parts

This is a point for women to remember if they have to play men's parts, and also the general principle that men move their arms more freely from the shoulder joint, and their legs from the hip joint; while women move from the elbow and the knee.

It is right for a man to stand with knees braced, feet apart, and his weight evenly on both feet, while it is more graceful for a woman to stand or sit with knees close together, and the weight on one leg, with the other relaxed. When a man has his weight on one leg, the knee of the other looks better bent outwards rather than inwards.

1	2
Right stance for a man.	Wrong (weak) stance for a man.

Men should be particularly careful to stand well when wearing tights or knee-breeches.

Exercises for Practice in Gesture

EXERCISE 13

Express (*a*) pleading or offering, first with both arms and hands, then with one hand only; (*b*) refusal and disappointment; (*c*) nervous apprehension; (*d*) sudden anger; (*e*) beckoning, and dismissal, with small and large movement; (*f*) horror, or disgust (fingers only); (*g*) groping in the dark, or in blindness; (*h*) deprecation.

Stage Falls

EXERCISE 14

One is frequently asked to demonstrate stage falls. This is a perfectly simple process, and quite painless, provided that the whole body is relaxed before it falls; that is essential. The body should reach the ground in the follow-

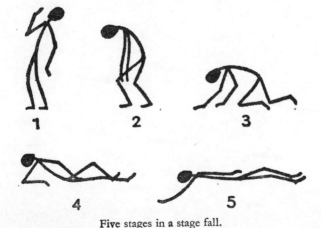

Five stages in a stage fall.

ing way: first knees, then hips, then shoulders, lastly head. Falls should be practised in slow motion at first:

1. Relax the body and sway backwards.
2. Then sway forwards.
3. Droop into a kneeling position.
4. Turn sideways from the hips, and lower the upper part of the body till first one shoulder, then the other, touches the ground.
5. Lower the head to the ground.

This can be practised with gradual increase of speed, until it appears almost instantaneous. The actor will not hurt himself if he remembers to round his shoulders, and keep his head forward when his shoulders reach the ground. Falls need very seldom be really sudden. It is usually possible, and more natural, to stagger for a few steps and then fall gradually. In any case, it is effective to sway backwards before falling forwards or sideways.

CHAPTER VII

A PLEA TO AUDIENCES

THE theatre has one thing to give which the cinema can never give, and that is the living contact between actors and audience at performance. The screen play is complete before it reaches the audience, and their reactions can in no way affect it: it cannot respond to tears, laughter, or applause—it cannot even wait for them. The stage play depends to a considerable extent, upon the co-operation of the audience for its success.

Everyone who has acted knows the thrill of hearing the murmur of voices from the unseen audience beyond the curtain, as he waits for the play to begin. Every playgoer knows the thrill of wondering what is behind that curtain, as he waits for it to rise. The moment it has risen, contact between actors and audience is established. The audience will give first their eyes and ears, later their mind, and at length perhaps their heart, in just the degree in which the actor gives his to them. It is for the actor to make the first move, to which the audience must respond; but if they fail to respond, the actor may get no further. There must be effort on both sides.

We have urged the amateur actor to learn his job; we have tried to impress on him the necessity of getting over his performance to the audience with clarity, and of making his presentation of a character interesting and varied; we have encouraged him to enlarge his range, and not to flinch from tackling strong emotional parts. But if he attempts to put all this into practice, what encouragement will he receive from his audience?

In a book on Etiquette, published in 1880, there is a

passage which says: "At amateur theatricals, do not openly express disapproval, but endeavour to endure them with patience." The manners of the modern audience hardly need such a reminder, but what do they give the amateur actor beyond polite attention? Do they appreciate his his desire to take his work seriously? Do they notice if he improves? Do they meet him half-way by responding to the atmosphere he is attempting to create? Do they listen to the words which he is trying to charge with meaning?

Judging fron the comments one hears from the audience at a great many amateur performances, they do not. However good the acting may be, the audience appear to take more interest in the personal identity of the actors as private individuals, than as characters in a story that is being unfolded.

When the play begins, one hears such comments and remarks as: "Is that Mrs. So-and-so's niece?" "That must be the young man I saw out with Betty Smith last weekend." "Fancy young Brown making love to Mrs. Jones! I wonder how Jones likes it?" "I don't think it's nice for a churchwarden to use language like that!" "Why, she's wearing Joan's frock—the one she had for the Hunt Ball last winter." "Mrs. Roberts looks quite pretty; I'd never have known her."

This sort of thing means that the play will be half over before anyone begins to listen to what the actors are saying, so great are the distractions bred by the blending of the familiar with the unfamiliar. If only audiences could interest themselves in the story of the play, and would concentrate less on the hat the actress is wearing and more on what she is saying from under it, the amateur actor's work would be considerably easier.

As it is, he has a harder task than the professional to make the character he is impersonating live in the minds of the audience. Sometimes audiences will go to the other extreme, and embarrass an actor by expecting him to remain in his stage character in private life. Shy young village actors have sometimes been so teased by their friends after a performance, or about their appearance in some particular part, that they could never be induced to act again.

One fully appreciates the difficulties with which an audience has to contend in receiving illusion. We have just seen Oberon arrive, in spectacles, on a motor bicycle. That very morning "a wood near Athens" was being used as a platform for a meeting of the Mothers' Union. Our children's bare legs suggest not so much fairies as colds in the head and drawing-pins in the feet. In Titania's sequined wings we recognize with a shock the evening wrap we had been hunting for before coming out. . . .

No; it is not easy, but we must try to accord to these actors "the willing suspension of disbelief", or we shall be left with nothing but "the theatre we deserve".

STAGE-MANAGEMENT

AN efficient and hard-working stage-manager is one of the most valuable assets an amateur company can possess, and such a person is too seldom to be found in the average dramatic society. This is sometimes because his function is not rightly understood, owing partly to the selfishness or short-sightedness of producers.

As long as the producer looks upon his stage-manager (hereafter to be referred to as the "S.M.") as a mere bottle-washer, to relieve him of the dirty work, there will continue to be a scarcity of candidates for the post. Stage-management is an arduous job, but can be intensely interesting to anyone who is practical and capable, provided that he is given his due share of responsibility in the production. He is not a luxury, but a necessity. No producer, however competent, can put on a show really satisfactorily without the help of an S.M.

Inexperienced producers do not realize this, and attempt to do too much themselves. How often one hears an amateur producer say after every show, "Yes, but it really was too much. I had to see to *everything*—props, clothes, scenery, lighting—every little thing. I couldn't possibly undertake it another year." (But he does.) In nine cases out of ten the martyred producer has only himself to blame for his troubles. He has not learnt to delegate authority, and he works under the mistaken impression that "he must see to everything himself, if he is to make sure that it really gets done". Unless he will hand over some of the interesting jobs to other people, and *trust them to do it*, he will never get any real assistance. No S.M.

will be interested in carrying out a job if he knows he is being watched all the time by someone who feels he could do it better himself.

Relations between Stage-Manager and Producer

The producer should take the S.M. into his confidence from the outset, and share his plans with him. The producer is, so to speak, "the brains", and the S.M. "the hands", of the production; the producer has the bright ideas, and the S.M. puts them into practice. The qualities of creative imagination and dramatic instinct are not essential in an S.M., nor is practical and organizing ability essential in a producer, but between them they should supply all these qualities, and the result should be a strong combination.

As soon as the producer has read and planned out the play, he should confer with his S.M., explain his scheme for the play to him, and discuss the kind of settings, lighting, costumes, and properties he will need. If the company boasts scenic and costume designers, they, too, will be present at the conference. They will later submit their designs to the producer, but it is the S.M. who will decide how they are to be carried out, and give instructions for the making of them. He will scour the neighbourhood for possible properties and costumes, and make notes as to where they may be begged or borrowed. He will draw up an estimate of the probable costs of production, and submit it to the business manager, or treasurer, and he will see that the expenditure on the show is kept within its limit.

It is sometimes the unpleasant duty of the S.M. to put a restraining hand on the fancy of the producer in order to keep his ideas within the bounds of economic possibility. If he is clever, he will devise simple ways by which

F

the producer can get the effect he wants by the maximum of suggestion and the minimum of outlay. He will realize that often imitation is actually more effective on the stage than reality; papier-mâché "food", once made, will last for many performances, and cost nothing but the price of a newspaper and a little time and trouble. A few penn'orth of gravy-browning, mixed with water, will readily be accepted as whisky or sherry—by the audience, if not by the actors. If a play has a large number of scenes, for which adequate sets cannot be provided, much can be done by judicious lighting. Let the bare essentials of the scene be picked out in a pool of light cast by a focus lamp, and the rest of the stage left in the doubt of darkness. A flexible and adaptable lighting set should be the aim of every S.M., from economical as well as artistic motives.

The Prompt Copy

Having discussed the plan of the play, the S.M. may then like to prepare a prompt-script of his own, or he may prefer to leave this to his assistant (the A.S.M.). A good, clear prompt-book is a useful thing to keep for reference, particularly if a production is likely to be revived at a later date, though often a great deal of time is wasted over neat diagrams, blue pencils, red ink, and the like, and a magnificent prompt copy is compiled, which no one ever looks at. The need for an exact prompt-book depends on the nature of the production. If it is an ordinary straight play, in which the printed stage-directions are being followed to a great extent, it is usually possible to write in all the necessary producer's instructions in the margin of the page. If the production is more elaborate, such as a Shakespearean, or other play in which no stage-directions are given, then a special prompt-book will be necessary.

There are many different methods of making a prompt-script. One is to interleave the printed book with blank pages—a tiresome business, which involves either unbinding and rebinding the book, or cutting sheets of paper a little smaller than the book's pages and pasting them on to the margin of each page, taking care not to cover up any of the printing.

A second way is to unbind the book, puncture each page with two holes, and put them into a loose-leaf notebook, with blank pages alternating. This is a quicker method, but the holes are apt to tear, and the pages come out if the book is not handled with care.

A third method is to have a duplicate copy of the book, and paste each page of the play on to the right-hand page of an exercise-book, leaving the left-hand page blank for notes. The duplicate is, of course, necessary, as the underneath side of the printed page cannot be used. This is, perhaps, the most durable and satisfactory method.

A fourth way is to have a typed copy made of the play, each act bound separately, and inter-leaved with blank pages. This is an expensive method.

In the prompt copy the S.M., or his assistant, records every movement given to the actors by the producer, and makes diagrams of the grouping, where necessary. He will also make a ground-plan of the stage and furniture for each act, and he will write "warning" and "go" signals opposite the appropriate cue, for all effects, such as "noises off", lighting changes, sound effects, and "curtains". A usual method is to indicate all such effects by a star (*), followed by the words (in red or blue chalk to make them catch the eye), "WARN Thunder"; then, lower down, "Thunder Go", or "WARN Curtain", and "Curtain Go". It is essential to put in the warning at the cue about half a page before the effect is due, or it is likely to be mistimed.

He will write in "calls" as well. For example, the words "Call Judith" will appear about two pages before Judith's entrance. The light-plot need not be included in the prompt-book; only light changes which occur on cue during the performance.

Rehearsal Calls

The next duty of the S.M. is to notify all members of the company as to the time, date, and place of the first rehearsal. In an amateur company it is more than ever essential that each member of the cast should receive *written* notice of each and every rehearsal. More amateur performances fail because of inadequate rehearsal than for any other reason. A tradition should be firmly established from the first that to miss a rehearsal, or come late —unless the S.M. has been notified—is an unpardonable offence. The S.M., on the other hand, must never fail in notifying the cast of rehearsals. It is not safe to trust to announcing it at a previous rehearsal, or to verbal or telephone messages. The "calls" should always be in writing. A good arrangement is to have a number of postcards printed, saying:

> "Your next rehearsal is on .... at......
> o'clock, in .... Please let me know
> if you are unable to attend.
> Signed..............................
> Stage-Manager."

It takes very little time to fill in the date and place of rehearsal, and the cost of printing some hundreds is small.

It is wise to study the convenience of the actors, and not to call them for eight o'clock if their scene is not likely to be taken till nine o'clock.

When the play is cast, the S.M. makes a separate list of

the names, addresses, and telephone numbers of all the people concerned—actors, understudies, designers, electricians, etc. This list should be kept at the back of his prompt-book.

At Rehearsal

At the first rehearsal the S.M. should be there at least half an hour before it is timed to begin, and with the help of the A.S.M. should set the stage for the scene to be rehearsed. He should place the necessary furniture in position. If the actual furniture to be used in performance is not available, something approximating to it should be provided. If the rehearsal is not on the stage, but in a room, he should indicate the dimensions of the stage by chalk marks on the floor, and exits and entrances should be marked by two chairs, between which the actors must make their entrance. Hand properties need not be provided at the first rehearsal, as actors can make little use of them while they have their scripts in their hands. They must, however, be provided by the second or third rehearsal, as the handling of properties greatly affects the timing of the play. Usually the A.S.M. is made responsible for hand props.

The S.M. must not Produce

At the first and every rehearsal the S.M. sits by the producer, noting in his book every movement and direction that is given to the actors, and making diagrams of the grouping of each scene. Then, in the absence of the producer, the S.M. is able to conduct rehearsals, but he should rehearse the company for "lines and business" only. He should never on any account make any suggestions as to interpretation. If he does so, he is bound to confuse the actors. Many S.M.'s are would-be producers, and the temptation to try their hand at producing, when given such an opportunity, is strong, but must be resisted.

A good S.M. can be of invaluable assistance in putting the cast through the mechanics of the play. Possibly the producer is not able to attend every rehearsal, and if the S.M. can carry on at one or two early rehearsals, get the framework of the play into shape, and help the actors with their lines, the producer, when he returns, can concentrate entirely on interpretation and polish.

The S.M. should rehearse the understudies. Understudies are apparently a luxury which very few amateur companies possess, mainly because few people are keen enough to learn a part and attend rehearsals when the chances of playing are slender. It is none the less essential to have understudies. Even if the play is only to be performed once, it is quite likely that a principal may break his leg the day before the show, and it is a fatal mistake for the producer to play the part, as so often happens. Understudies are useless unless rehearsed, and they are more likely to be interested if they are rehearsed.

Prompting

The prompter, who is usually the A.S.M., should be present at all rehearsals. Sometimes the S.M. undertakes the prompting, but that is unwise, particularly if there are "effects" and such things to be superintended during the show. Prompting at a first performance is a full-time job, and the prompter should have no other duties to distract him. It is a difficult and rather a thankless task, but interesting, and a really good prompter is a godsend to a company. The prompter must be present at rehearsals in order to know exactly how the play goes; when there are pauses for effect, or for business; and, above all, when the actors are likely to need prompting. Oddly enough, an actor nearly always "dries up" at the same place, and such places should be marked with a danger signal in the prompt copy.

The prompter should follow the text very closely, preferably running a pencil along the lines as they are spoken, so that if his attention is distracted for a moment he can quickly find his place again by the position of the pencil. It is a mistake to read out the lines in a whisper, as the French do; it is most distracting to the actors. The prompter must be able to distinguish between "fluffing" —a temporary hesitation, when the actor cannot remember the exact word he wants—and "drying up", when the actor's mind has become a complete blank, and he will probably lose his head. In the case of fluffing, it is usually enough to supply the actor with the missing word, and the prompt should be so timed that the prompter's voice is heard exactly on the syllable where it is wanted. If the prompter has not been following closely, one sometimes hears the harassed actor exclaim, "I've said that!" The prompter can usually tell from the actor's face when he needs prompting. The experienced actor will throw a glance at the prompt-corner when he wants a line. In the case of a "dry up", the prompter will have to give more than a word, and should say the lines, clearly and distinctly, until the actor picks them up again.

The loudness of the prompter's voice needs careful judgment. It is a pity if the audience can hear him, but it is better that he should prompt rather too loudly, once, than that the actor should not hear him, and that he should have to prompt repeatedly. The ideal prompter has a low but carrying voice. The most difficult problem for the prompter, which requires a steady head and quick judgment, is when the actors miss out a large piece of dialogue. He must then decide quickly whether the omission is going to damage the coherence of the play and upset the actors, or whether it does not matter. If something vital has been left out, the prompter must immediately break in by prompting *the line the actor ought to have said* before he skipped. Quite likely the actor does not realize that he has left something out, but if he hears the prompter's voice saying a line he has not said, he will quickly be recalled.

If the actors have confidence in the prompter, and know that he is familiar with the play, and their playing of it, it will have a steadying effect on their acting at a first performance. The prompter should always be stationed on the "prompt side", which is the actor's *left*, as that is where the actor expects to hear him.

At the Show

As the production approaches performance, the work and responsibility of the S.M. increase. It is for him to see that conditions for the dress rehearsal are exactly as for a performance, and at the performance itself the S.M. takes entire charge of the production. The work of the producer is finished, for better or for worse, and he must then hand over to the S.M., and not come near the stage until the show is over. He should be in front, among the audience, watching the performance, and taking notes. The S.M. has the right to forbid him access to the stage.

The S.M. must see that the stage is ready, and that all scenery, furniture, and props are in their right places, and checked by his list. A good S.M. keeps his property list, light-plot, and stage plan in his head, and does not depend on a list, which might be mislaid at the last moment; but it is wise to have such a list for reference.

The A.S.M. should look after the hand props. Those which are brought on by the actors should be kept on a table in the wings, handed to the actor as he goes on, and taken from him again when he comes off. It is better not to let the actors be responsible for their own personal props. If one person only is responsible for all, there should be no doubt or confusion as to where the things are to be found.

Half an hour before the performance is timed to begin, the S.M. should send the A.S.M., or some other helper, to warn the actors. This person should call out, "Half an hour, please", then "Quarter of an hour, please", then "Five minutes, please", and finally, "Beginners, please", in every dressing-room. A call-boy is a luxury, but amateurs love to be called. It makes them feel, "This is Real Theatre!"—even if there is only one dressing-room to be called. Apart from its psychological value, it has a steadying effect on the actors' nerves to be told exactly how much time they have.

If there is an overture, or *entr'acte* music, the S.M. should know how long to allow for this, and should give the signal for the orchestra to begin, say seven minutes before the curtain rises. The usual signal is a red light on the conductor's stand, operated from the switchboard in the prompt-corner, but if this is impossible it is advisable to have a small bell, or buzzer, which is audible to the orchestra but not to the whole auditorium.

When the actors are called, and in their places, the stage-lighting should be put on, and the following signals should be given:

1. "House-lights."
2. "Going up."
3. "Curtain up."

1. It is essential to remember to switch off the house-lights before ringing up, as this concentrates the attention of the audience on the stage, and the S.M. must always

remember to put them on again the moment the final curtain is down on each act.

2. It is very necessary to warn the actors before raising the curtain. Otherwise it may rise to reveal the legs of a stage-hand, or other unwanted person, scuttling off the stage, or an actor hastily concealing his part behind his newspaper.

3. *Never ring up more than five minutes later than the time the show is advertised to start*, whether the audience is in or not. It is discourteous to those members of the audience who have arrived in good time to keep them waiting, and once a company has acquired a reputation for starting late, the audience will never attempt to be punctual.

As soon as the curtain is up the S.M. should make a note of the time, and note the time again at the conclusion of the act. This is a check on the pace of the play. A play should play roughly at the rate of a typescript page a minute, so a thirty-page act should play about thirty minutes, and if it is found to take fifty minutes, something will have to be done about it, and the actors can be warned to keep the pace going in Act II.

When the curtain is down on Act I, and the house-lights up, the S.M. should clear the stage of actors, and superintend the scene-shift. He must be ruthless, and will probably be very unpopular in his efforts to keep the actors off the stage, and wings before, and during, the play, as well as in the intervals. As a rule, the moment the curtain is down the actors will rush together, exclaiming excitedly, "My dear, *did* you see what happened in the tea-party scene?" or, "Do you think they noticed that frightful dry-up when I thought my beard was coming off?" They must be shooed firmly to their dressing-rooms, so that the stage-staff can get on with the changing of the set. Nor should anyone be allowed in the wings

while the acts are playing, except the actors awaiting
their cues, and the strictest silence should be maintained.

Scene-shifts must be Rehearsed

It is important that intervals should be timed, and not
prolonged. Long waits will try the patience of the
audience, and do much to damage the success of the performance. In order to ensure short intervals, scene-shifts
must be carefully rehearsed and timed. If the available
wing-space is small, the storing of the props and furniture
must be worked out exactly, and the scene-shifters must
know exactly where everything is to be put. One or two
efficient helpers are of more use than a whole army of
zealous but uninstructed assistants. The golden rule of
scene-shifting is, "*Bring on before you take off*". As soon as
the curtain is down, the furniture should be assembled
in the middle of the stage, in order to free the flats, and the
furniture for Act II should be brought on and placed in
the middle of the stage, before the Act I stuff is removed.
Otherwise, unless the wing-space is very extensive, it will
probably be found that the grand piano used in Act I has
been put on top of the cake-stand wanted in Act II. If it is
possible to keep all the Act II props on the right of the
stage, and all the Act I props on the left of the stage, then
the Act II things can be brought on at the same time as
the Act I things are removed, which is much quicker.

The position of each piece of furniture should be indicated by chalk marks on the stage. This is particularly
important on a small stage, where every inch counts, and
a wrong angle may upset the grouping and movements of
the players throughout the act. It is helpful to mark the
positions for Act I in white chalk, Act II in red chalk, and
Act III in blue chalk.

When the scene is set, the actors will be called, and the

three signals given as before. Some people like to use three strokes on a gong, or three knocks on the floor, for the signals. On the first stroke, the house-lights go out; the second warns the actors; and the third takes the curtain up. This method is not a suitable preliminary for every type of play. The rather sinister sound of a gong or a thump seems to suggest the approach of tragedy or melodrama, and is a little pretentious before a farce or a one-act comedy.

Curtain Calls

At the end of a play it is for the S.M. to arrange the number of curtain calls to be taken. If there are to be calls, they should be taken with a certain seemliness and dignity. The actors should be told in what positions they are to stand, and should remain in those positions, and bow, when the curtain goes up. The S.M. should make sure that they get quickly into their places before he takes the curtain up, or the audience may be presented with an empty stage, and the actors rush on just as the curtain falls; or else there may be a sheepish group of people, coyly nudging each other in one corner.

Artistically, curtain calls are inexcusable, but they have a psychological effect upon the audience. A skilful S.M., by manipulating the curtain quickly up and down, may be able to rouse the audience to a pitch of enthusiasm which will bring the play to such a glorious conclusion, that many previous shortcomings in the performance will be forgotten. He must make sure, though, that the curtain *will* rise and fall quickly. This, more than anything, needs rehearsal. Nine amateur curtains out of ten can be pulled briskly once, but no more. The rope sags, the curtain sticks, and can thereafter be manipulated only by hand. Nothing can be more shattering to illusion than to be unable to conclude an act with a curtain. The corpse that has to rise and walk away; the start of surprise that has to be "held" to wobbling-point; the stage embrace that has to be prolonged beyond the limits of decency, are too frequent calamities. In the case of such emergencies the S.M. should always remember to "black out".

The S.M. will greatly help the popularity of his company if he superintends the clearing-up of the stage, and the restoration of borrowed property, after the show.

A great deal of the success of a performance depends upon its "slickness". The audience can forgive lack of talent, and the shortcomings due to inexperience in the actors, but they cannot, nor should they be expected to, overlook faults on the mechanical side of the production, which could be avoided by common sense and taking trouble. The responsibility for this rests mainly with the S.M., and to him should be given the credit of a show which goes without a hitch. His difficulties will be less if he bears in mind the axiom:

"See to everything a *fortnight* before you think it necessary."

LIST OF RECOMMENDED BOOKS

ACTING

Stanislavski	*An Actor Prepares*	(Bles) (TAB)*
Redgrave	*The Actor's Ways &*	(Heinemann)
	Means	(TAB)
Saint-Denis	*Theatre: The Redis-*	(Heinemann)
	covery of Style	(TAB)
Fishman	*The Actor in Training*	(Jenkins)
Marowitz	*The Method as Means*	(Jenkins)
Lewis	*Method or Madness?*	(Heinemann)
		(French)
Seyler and	*The Craft of Comedy*	(Garnet Miller)
Haggard		(TAB)
Newton	*Exercise Improvisation*	(Garnet Miller)

SPEECH

Thurburn	*Voice and Speech*	(Nisbet)
Turner	*Voice and Speech*	(Nisbet)
	in the Theatre	(Pitman)
Bruford	*Speech and Drama*	(Methuen)

MOVEMENT

Oxenford	*Design for Movement*	(Garnet Miller)
		(TAB)
Bruford	*Teaching Mime*	(Methuen)

MAKE-UP

Thomas	*Make-up: the Dramatic*	(Garnet Miller)
	Student's Approach	(TAB)
Ward	*A Book of Make-up*	(French)
Stanley	*Guide to Grease-paint*	(French)

These books can be obtained from the British Drama League Library, 9 Fitzroy Square, London, W.1 (members only) and from Public Libraries.

---

* The second publisher is the American where the work is published in the United States. TAB = Theatre Arts Books.

EXERCISES

THESE Exercises were written for British Drama League courses in Drama. They are intended to illustrate many of the points dealt with in this book and to help the actor to acquire self-confidence; to develop his stage-sense; and to meet his need for practice in technique. Producers may like to devote the first quarter of an hour of rehearsal to practice of this kind.

The notes and suggestions are for the teacher or producer, to use or ignore, and have been placed at the end of each exercise in order not to confuse the actors as they read the scene.

Throughout this book the terms "left" and "right", applied to the stage, refer to the actor's left or right as he faces the audience. "Up stage" denotes the back of the stage, and "down stage" the front of the stage.

C. = Centre.	R. = Right.
L. = Left.	U. = Upper and Up Stage.

MAKING ENTRANCES AND EXITS

EXERCISE 15

OPENING AND CLOSING A SCENE

SCENE.—*A Sitting-room*

[*The only necessary furniture is a tea-table down* L., *and chairs* R. *and* L. *of it. The* HOSTESS *is seated on chair down* L., *below table. The* GUEST *enters* U.R.]

[*Enter* MAID.]

MAID [*announcing*]: Mrs. Smith, ma'am.

[*Mrs. Smith enters.*]

HOSTESS: Oh, how are you, my dear? I'm so glad you have come (1).

MRS. SMITH: Yes. I've been wanting to see you about this business (2) of Molly and John.

HOSTESS: Do sit down (3). You'll have some tea, won't you?

MRS. SMITH: No, thanks. I've just had some.

[*Here a conversation of some length is supposed to take place.*]

Well, I am afraid I must be going (4).

HOSTESS: So nice of you to have come (5).

MRS. SMITH: I'm very glad I found you in. Good-bye.

HOSTESS: Good-bye. Give my love to Molly and John.

MRS. SMITH: I will. Good-bye.

NOTES

This is an exercise for attack and pace in the opening and closing of a scene in a modern straight play. The lines themselves are relatively unimportant, but the point is that they must flow briskly, in order to cover the necessary business and movements, without any halting or pauses.

1. The Hostess should advance to meet the Guest, *speaking as she goes, and should meet her about centre stage*. She should then turn to the left and walk back towards the table, indicating the chair for the visitor with her right hand as she passes it.

2. This line is presumably "plot", and therefore must be given rather more weight than the others.

3. On this line the hostess will have got back to her chair, and should sit as she says it.

4. Rise on this line.

5. Move to Guest and walk with her to the door, *speaking all the time*, so that the final "good-bye" of Mrs. Smith is said off, the Hostess looking after her through the door.

The attack and pace of the scene must be vigorous and brisk, without giving the appearance of being hurried, and the actors must remember to project their voice and personality.

EXERCISE 16

(Alternative version of Exercise 15, for Men.)

SCENE.—*Desk and chairs down* L., *as in Exercise* 15.
Entrance up R.

[*Enter* CLERK, U.R.]

CLERK: Mr. Smith to see you, sir.

BROWN: All right. Show him in.   [*Exit* CLERK.

CLERK [*re-enter immediately! announcing*]: Mr. Smith.

BROWN: Ah, Smith, how are you?

SMITH: Quite well, thanks. I called to see you about this Manchester business.

BROWN: Yes? Sit down, won't you? Have a cigarette?

SMITH: No, thanks. I don't smoke.

.   .   .   .   .   .

SMITH: Well, I must be off. Glad we've fixed it up.

BROWN: Yes, I'm glad you came. Good-bye.

G

SMITH: Good-bye. Remember me to your wife.

BROWN: Thanks, I will. Good-bye.

[*Note.*—Producers should try this exercise with the furniture and entrance arranged in different positions, and notice how the pace and timing of the scene is affected.]

EXERCISE 17

SCENE.—*A Parlour. Period about* 1830.

[*Tea-table and* HOSTESS'*s chair down* L. *Chair* R. *of table, and settee down* R.]

[*Enter* MAID, U.R.]

MAID [*announcing*]: Miss Graham, ma'am, and Miss Laetitia Graham.　[*Enter the* MISSES GRAHAM.]

HOSTESS: Ah, my dear Fanny! (1) This is indeed a pleasure (2), and Miss Letty, too (3).

MISS G.: Dear Anna!

LETTY: Good afternoon, Miss Anna (4).

HOSTESS: Pray be seated, and I beg that you will join me in a dish of tea (5).

MISS G.: You are very kind (6).

LETTY: Most kind (7).

NOTES

This scene is similar to Exercise 15, but the movements and general pace of the scene are affected by the period. The manipulation of full skirts or crinolines will make the timing somewhat slower, but still the dialogue must be smooth and continuous.

1. All curtsy on this line.
2. Kissing Miss Graham.
3. Kissing Miss Letty.

4. This line should be spoken simultaneously with Miss Graham's "Dear Anna". Miss Letty must enter and remain below Miss Graham, on her right.

5. Movements exactly as in Exercise 15. See Note 1.

6. Sitting on chair R. of table.

7. Sitting on settee.

EXERCISE 18

WORKING UP TO AN ENTRANCE

SCENE.—*A Cottage Interior*

[*Entrance back* C. *Fireplace down* L. *Chairs above it and below it, but on the oblique, with the upstage chair slightly towards* C. *and not masked by lower chair. Table down* R.]

[MOTHER *sits in upstage chair.* BESS *in lower chair, three-quarters of her back to the audience.*]

BESS: Well, I shall be glad when it's settled one way or the other (1).

MOTHER: Aye, it's worrying not hearing anything. Well, Bess, it's getting late; we'd best be going to bed.

[*Knock* (2).]

BESS: Who can that be at this time of night?

MOTHER [*goes to door and unlocks it*] (3): Jenny!

JENNY: I've come back, Mother. It's all over (4).

NOTES

This is an exercise in the timing of an entrance. Try playing the scene, (*a*) as if Jenny were bringing good news; and (*b*) as if she were bringing bad news, and note the difference in the timing.

1. Bess should express her uneasiness in her voice, her movements, and the attitude in which she sits.

2. Here both should start, and there should be a definitely marked pause, during which the two women exchange frightened glances.

3. Mother opens door from right to left so as to clear Jenny, who is revealed outlined in the doorway.

4. If playing the scene for (*a*) Jenny should go straight to her mother, speaking as she goes. If for (*b*) she should walk down to table R., the others watching her intently, place hat or gloves on table before speaking, and then speak in a toneless voice, looking straight in front of her, not at either of the women. This is "subjective" playing. The other (*a*) is "objective". Attention should be paid to the *direction of the eyes* of the players throughout the scene.

Try setting this scene with entrance L. or R., and note the difference it makes to timing, grouping, and general effect.

EXERCISE 19

TIMING IN MAKING AN EXIT

SCENE.—*Any setting*.

[A. *is sitting down* L. B. *is right of* C. *Exit is up* R.]

B.: Then you won't tell me where you were last night?
A.: No.
B.: I strongly advise you to do so (1).
A.: I refuse, absolutely (2).
B.: Very well, then: there is nothing more to be said (3). But I warn you, you have not heard the last of this (4) —by any means.　　　　　　　　　　　　　　　　　[*Exit*.

NOTES

1. On this line B. should advance on A., close up to him, in a threatening manner.

2. On this line A. should rise and confront B., face to face (contracted movement for both). They should hold this position during a pause of about two seconds. The actors should feel form and significance in the pause.

3. Relaxed attitude and a change of manner, implying a change of idea, should occur on this line. After this sentence B. should turn sharply on his heel to his right, and cross briskly to the door. There he should pause and say the last sentence from the door, and on the words "by any means" should slam the door sharply. A sentence delivered thus on the exit, and finished with an abrupt movement, such as slamming the door, gives point and slickness to a "strong" exit.

4. Try crossing to the exit after this line and delivering only the words "by any means" at the door, and decide which method is the more effective.

EXERCISE 20

For Timing of Exit and Team Work

Scene.—*A Cottage Interior.*

[*Table* C. Mother *seated at it*, C. Mrs. Jones, R. *of it.* Elsie, *standing close to* Mother, R. *of her. Exit up* R.]

Elsie: Well, Mother, I don't care what you say. I'm fond of Harry, and I'm going to give him the answer he wants tonight. Good-bye, Mrs. Jones. I'm off to meet Harry now (1).

Mother: Wait, Elsie!

Elsie: No, Mother, my mind's made up (2).

[*Exit* Elsie.

Mrs. Jones: Well, there now!

Mother: She's a headstrong lass, and she won't listen to me.

MRS. JONES: Aye, they're both over young. But it's no use us setting ourselves up against them.

NOTES

1. Elsie moves towards door on this line.
2. Brisk exit, as in Exercise 19. Both the other women should turn and stare after her, and there should be a considerable pause before they resume the dialogue, while the women continue to hold their position. This should be carefully timed. If the dialogue is resumed too soon, Elsie's exit will be "killed". This is an example of team-playing.

EXERCISE 21

FOR TIMING OF ENTRANCE OF A GROUP OF PEOPLE

SCENE.—*A Cottage Interior.*

PERIOD.—*French Revolution* 1790.

[B *is seated down* L. *There is a window, curtained,* C. *Entrance up* R.]

[A., C., D., E., *and* F. *are revolutionaries;* B. *is the owner of the cottage.*]

[*Angry murmurs are heard off, and then knocking on the door.*]

A. [*off*]: Open in the name of the Republic!

B. [*goes to open door* (1), *then retreats,* L.C.]: What do you want?

A.: The Princess—we saw her come in here (2).

C.: She must be here.

D.: You'd better give her up.

E.: Cursed aristocrat!

F.: What's behind that curtain?

NOTES

The effect to be aimed at in this scene is a confused and angry murmur of sound from the Revolutionaries. They should not wait for their cues, but should speak their lines almost simultaneously as they enter, but F.'s line must stand out. B. is presumably hiding the aristocrat refugee behind the window-curtains.

1. B. should hesitate and show fear before going to the door, and should cast an anxious glance in the direction of the window.

2. The Revolutionaries should rush in in a mob, and group themselves obliquely across the stage R., but not in a straight line. A. should be a couple of paces in front of the rest. F. should be the farthest down stage, so that he is clearly seen by the audience and has a clear line of vision in the direction of the window.

THE USE OF THE PAUSE

THE TIMING OF BUSINESS

EXERCISE 22

SCENE.—*Any Setting.*

Start here [A. *is seated* R. B. *is leaning against table, down* L.]

A.: Let me see that letter.

B.: No, I don't want you to.

A.: Let me see that letter (1).

B.: It's nothing really. I don't know why I said anything about it, only . . .

A.: Who wrote this?

over

NOTES

The use of the pause will be quite different according to whether the scene is of (*a*) trivial, or (*b*) grave importance.

1. (*a*) If the scene is being played lightly, and the letter contains nothing of particular importance, and A. is merely coaxing B. to show it to him, B. should cross to A. on this cue and hand him the letter, *speaking as he goes*.

(*b*) If the scene is serious, A. will *command* B. to show him the letter, and B. will finally submit, against his will. In this case there will be a pause here, and then B. will cross to A. *in silence*, the movement thereby standing out as significant. He will take up his next speech hastily, while A, is reading the letter.

Remember that when speech and movement coincide, neither can be particularly significant. Movement will detract attention from an important speech; similarly, if speech ceases when a movement is made, the attention of the audience will be concentrated on the movement. Therefore, when there is "business" of a trivial nature, such as the handing of cups of tea on the stage, the movements should be covered by the lines of the dialogue.

Exercise 23

Scene.—*A Cottage Kitchen*

[*Table* C., *chair* L. *of it.* MOTHER *by fireplace down* L. *Entrance back* C. *Dresser up stage* R.C.]

[*Enter* DAUGHTER.]

MOTHER: Well, my dear, you're late. I've kept some tea for you (1).

DAUGHTER: Thanks (2).

MOTHER: It'll soon boil up again. Try some of that cake

(3), and come and sit the side nearest the fire (4). You look tired (5) . . . not worrying about anything, are you? (6).

DAUGHTER: No.

MOTHER: Here's your tea, freshly made (7).

DAUGHTER: Thanks.

MOTHER: Seen Arthur today? (8).

DAUGHTER: No . . . he . . . Oh, damn everything (9)! . . . [*Bursts into tears.*] [*Exit.*

NOTES

1. Mother replaces kettle on fire as she speaks this line.
2. Daughter is standing behind table C.
3. Mother goes to table and draws cake to L. of table as she speaks.
4. Motions daughter to chair L. of table. Draws out chair, and daughter moves to it, crossing between table and chair. Mother is standing behind the chair, watching daughter intently. She then crosses to dresser, brings pot of jam, and places it on table by daughter, casting an anxious glance at her daughter from time to time. There is silence during these movements. The mother is always behind the daughter, so that the audience can see the expression on her face, but the daughter cannot.
5. This line is said as she places the jam on the table. There is another pause, during which the mother crosses to the fireplace again.
6. This line is said as the mother is lifting the kettle off the fire, the movement being intended deliberately to hide the anxiety which lies behind the question.
7. Crossing with kettle behind daughter to table.
8. Pouring hot water into teapot on table.
9. She jumps up and runs to the door on this line.

The daughter should speak all her lines quietly and tonelessly, until her sudden outburst at the end.

Exercise 24

Building Up Climax

Scene.. *A Sitting-room.*

[MOTHER *and* AUNT EDITH *are seated on a settee down* R. *There is a table with a telephone upon it down* L.]

MOTHER: Yes, I am glad they are settled. Somehow I had not expected it would be Harry.

AUNT EDITH: No; Joan had so many young men (1); but we all hoped it would be Harry. . . . You must miss Joan dreadfully.

MOTHER: I do, of course; but they are not so very far away. They quite often come over for the day, or the week-end.

AUNT EDITH: That is nice for you. . . .

[*Enter* HARRY, *up* L.]

MOTHER: Why, hallo, Harry! This is a surprise visit. . . . You know Joan's Aunt Edith, don't you? (2).

HARRY: Yes, how do you do? [*Shakes hands, then turns to* MOTHER.] I've called for Joan. Is she about ready, do you think?

MOTHER: Joan? But she isn't here!

HARRY: Not here? (3). When did she leave?

MOTHER: She has not been here. I've not seen her since last week-end.

HARRY: Do you mean to say she has not been spending the day here?

MOTHER: No . . . why? . . . Did she? . . .

HARRY: She told me this morning she was coming here, and I said I'd fetch her back tonight. It's queer. . . . She must have changed her mind. . . . I'll just ring up home and see if she's back. . . . [*Goes to phone.*] Hallo!

... Primrose, 4401, please.... Hallo! ... are you there? Has Mrs. Chilton come back yet? ... Oh (4) ... Has there been any message from her? ... No ... Yes, Mr. Chilton speaking.... Good-bye.... She's not there.

MOTHER: What can have happened, Harry? [*Pause.*] There's nothing wrong, is there?

HARRY: N-no, I don't think so.... We had a bit of a row ... and ... I wonder. I think I'll go back now. She'll probably turn up by the time I get there.... Good-bye. Good-bye, Aunt Edith....   [*Hurries to door.*

MOTHER [*after him*]: But, Harry, you must let me know when she comes back. I don't like. ...

HARRY [*off*]: Yes, yes. I'll ring up.

[MOTHER *comes slowly back, and she and* AUNT *exchange glances.*]

NOTES

1. This is a "plot line", and must be pointed accordingly. It has been proved possible to play the part of Aunt Edith for comedy. An acid rendering of this line can suggest this, and also her demeanour throughout the scene, culminating in the way in which she exchanges glances with the mother at the end. It is an interesting experiment in team acting to see how far the part can be developed on these lines without detracting sympathy from Harry or weakening the dramatic value of the scene.

2. This line is an indication that Harry is too much preoccupied to notice Aunt Edith when he first comes in. He must therefore avoid looking at her until this moment.

3. Harry must be careful not to register too much surprise and shock at this point. He must keep something in reserve, in order to work up to a climax.

4. Harry's anxiety should reach its climax here, and remain at that level until the end of the scene.

CONTRAST IN CHANGE OF MOOD

EXERCISE 25

(Note that change of mood will imply a change in tone and pace.)

SCENE.—*A Draper's Shop.*

[*Table or counter down* L. *Shop window runs across the back of the stage. Entrance up* L. SMITH *is standing* C., *with one foot upon a chair, in an easy, swaggering attitude.* MATHER *is* R. *of him.*]

SMITH: Well, I've never let anyone come it over me, and I'm not going to start now. If young Carter thinks he can order me about like a dog, he's very much mistaken. Next time he comes interfering in my department, I intend to show him where he gets off.

MATHER: That's right.

SMITH: Does he think I don't know my job? Why, I was in the drapery business before he was born, and I've forgotten more about textiles then he ever knew.

MATHER: I'm sure you have (1).

SMITH: Eh? . . . Anyhow, I'm not going to put up with it a day longer. Next time he gives me an order I shall just look at him and say . . .

[*Enter* Carter (2).]

CARTER: Smith, you might take these samples over to Mr. Roberts, and tell him I've O.K'd them. [*Throws patterns on table* L.] And when you come back, get that window smartened up. It looks a bit fly-blown.

SMITH: Yes, Mr. Carter.

CARTER: Come along, Mather, I want you upstairs.

[MATHER *crosses behind* CARTER *to exit.*

And oh, Smith, as you go down, tell them to send up my tea, will you?

SMITH: Yes, Mr. Carter (3).

[*Exeunt* CARTER *and* MATHER. SMITH *picks up patterns and follows.*]

NOTES

1. Note that this line can be said in two quite different ways, suggesting either admiration or mocking. In either case the "Eh?" following should be said with a quick, suspicious glance at Mather, followed by an infinitesimal pause.

2. It is essential that Carter's entrance should be so timed that his opening line cuts in sharply on the word "say". At the sound of his voice the attitude of the two men should change quickly to one of respectful attention.

3. Smith must make a marked contrast between this and his earlier manner. The part can be played in two ways. Either Smith can climb down completely, in which case he would hurry meekly off with the patterns at the end; or else he can suggest suppressed anger and defiance in his attitude throughout the scene, in which case he might fling down the patterns and hold an attitude of defiance till the curtain comes down, glaring in the direction of the departed Carter in impotent rage.

EXERCISE 26

SCENE.—*Interior of a London Flat.*

TIME.—*August* 1914.

[MARY *sits* R. *of stage*, ANNE L. *There is a window back* C.]

ANNE: My dear, it was simply too *marvellous*! We stayed there till daylight, then Johnny got his car out, and we all packed in—Archie, and Bunny, and Bill and myself, and drove out to . . .

MARY: Listen (1)!

VOICE [*newspaper boy passing along street outside*]: England declares war! England declares war! England declares war!

MARY: War (2)!

ANNE: War!

MARY: I have nothing left to lose ... (3) But you ...

ANNE [*going to her*]: Mary, I'm frightened!

NOTES

This scene will only be effective if the part of the older woman, Mary, is played with great restraint. A touch of over-acting or theatricality in her playing would ruin it. She should use no gesture, and very little movement. In order to get contrast, Anne should project her opening speech with rather exaggerated brightness.

1. Here Mary can rise, and go up to the window to listen. As she stands there, the expression on her face should be visible to the audience. Alternatively, she can play the whole scene sitting where she is.

2. The point of the scene lies in the way the word "war" is spoken by the two women. Mary's should be very quiet, with a weight of recollection behind it. Anne's should suggest excitement and questioning, as though she were thinking, "How thrilling! Will it be fun?" Mary should come slowly down stage before she speaks, not looking at Anne, but lost in her own reflections.

3. This line also should be said very simply and gravely, and Mary is still not looking at Anne. (Subjective playing, see Exercise 18.) She turns her eyes and looks at Anne before she says, "But you ..." and it is at this point, and not till then, that there is a complete change of mood in Anne, as she goes to the older woman for protection.

EXERCISE 27

SCENE.—*A Parlour.*

TIME.—*Early Victorian Period.*

[*French window back* C. *Settee down* R. *Armchair* L. *Entrance* U.R. AMELIA *is sitting on settee.*]

LUCY: And he says I *must* let him know when I am going to Dawlish, so that he can try to arrange to get leave and be there at the same time. Amelia, when *are* we going? (1).

AMELIA: I don't know, my dear; you had better ask Papa (2).

LUCY: Yes . . . but I don't want him to guess . . .

[*Enter* PAPA (3).]

PAPA: Why is tea not ready? Where is your mother? I wish to speak to her (4).

AMELIA: Shall I find her, Papa?   [*Exit* (5).

LUCY: Dear Papa, you looked tired. You are in need of a holiday (6).

PAPA: True. But I shall not get it. I have come to the conclusion that it will be unwise to pay our annual visit to Devonshire this summer.

LUCY: Not go away . . .? (7).

PAPA: No. As things are at present, I feel it would be an unjustifiable extravagance?

LUCY: Not go to Dawlish?

PAPA: No.

LUCY: But we *always* go.

PAPA: I have told you we are not going. Now, leave me. I wish to talk to your mother.

[*Exit* LUCY *by french window*, C.

NOTES

1. On this line Lucy sits on the settee beside her sister. Remember that the movement will be affected by the full skirt, or crinoline.

2. This line could be said in two ways, suggesting either that Amelia really does not know; or that she knows, but dare not say, that they are not going.

3. Both daughters should rise at Papa's entrance. Lucy's movement should suggest fear that she may have been overheard.

4. Papa crosses straight to his chair and sits as he speaks this line.

5. Amelia, by a glance at Lucy at this exit, might suggest either encouragement or apprehension.

6. As Lucy speaks this line she crosses to behind her father's chair and stands there, so that both his face and hers are clearly visible to the audience, but they never look at each other.

7. It is effective if this and Lucy's two following speeches are spoken in the same tone of dazed dismay, as if she were thinking aloud. (Subjective playing.) The change of mood from eager hope to deep disappointment should not come till her exit, and should be expressed by the actress's back. She goes at first slowly, and then bursts into tears and runs out.

EXERCISE 28

SCENE.—*A Cottage Interior*.

[*Door* C. LIZZIE *sits* L. (1). *Enter* JIM.]

LIZZIE: Oh, there you are, Jim. I thought you was never coming. Where shall we go? There's a good picture on at the Regent.
JIM: I ain't going to no pictures (2).

LIZZIE: Why not? (3).
JIM: I got the sack.
LIZZIE: What? (4) . . . What for? (5).
JIM: Stealing.
LIZZIE: Jim! (6).

NOTES

1. Before Jim enters, Lizzie should show that she is eagerly anticipating his arrival, and is made anxious by his lateness. She jumps up when he appears, and when he has come down to centre stage, goes up to him and slips her arm through his.

2. Jim remains dull and shamefaced throughout, and avoids meeting her eyes.

3. A reaction of surprise, indicated by a slight contraction and drawing away of the body, without moving the feet.

4. A bigger reaction. She should retreat two or three steps away from him (contracted movement).

5. A step or body-movement towards him on this.

6. The greatest reaction and change of mood comes on this line, which might be interpreted in various ways, according to the wish of the actress. In any case, the first reaction would probably be a big movement away from Jim.

EXERCISE 29

(For change of mood and the playing of "dual" moods; anxiety masked by forced cheerfulness.)

SCENE.—*Any interior.*
[*Armchair by fire* R. ALICE *on settee* L. *She gets up on* BEN's *entrance.*]

ALICE: Oh, hallo, Ben!
BEN: Hallo, Alice. [*He kisses her perfunctorily* (1).]
ALICE: Had a busy day? (2).

H

BEN: Yes, fairly . . . I say, Alice, would you mind awfully if we didn't go out tonight? . . . Couldn't we have a cosy evening here instead—just you and I together? (3).

ALICE: Yes, of course, if you'd rather . . . I'd love that. . . . Anything the matter, Ben? You're feeling all right, aren't you?

BEN: Rather! I'm perfectly all right—just a bit of a head—nothing much. . . . Come here, darling. . . . I'm glad we're not going out; it'll be lovely to . . .

ALICE: Oh, by the way, there was a phone message for you—a Mr. Slade rang up. He wanted to see you . . .

BEN: Slade! (4).

ALICE: Yes; I told him I was expecting you soon after six, and he said he'd come round . . .

BEN [*jumping up*]: No! He can't! . . . I . . . Oh, God! Alice, I . . . (5).

[*Rushes from the room.*

NOTES

1. Alice remains on the settee. After kissing her, Ben crosses and sits in the armchair, his back slightly turned to her.

2. On this line Alice should show by her facial expression that she already guesses that something is wrong.

3. In this and Ben's next speech the two moods must be apparent. Alice has two "hidden" moods: disappointment, as well as anxiety.

4. Horror, fear, and dismay must be expressed here.

5. This speech must build up to an hysterical climax.

CREATION OF ATMOSPHERE AND CLIMAX

Exercise 30

Scene.—*A Room in an Empty House.*

[*It is empty save for a table* R., *and a large packing-case beside it. The door is down* L. A. *has been in the room before;* B. *has not.*]

[*Enter A., followed by B. A. turns on the light, then walks briskly to table, and lays his hat and gloves on it.*]

B.: I hope they'll come soon. I don't like this place; it gives me the creeps. Does anyone live here?

A. [*sitting on packing-case*]: No. It hasn't been occupied for years. They say it's haunted (1).

B.: I can well believe it. [*Comes and sits by A. on case.*] You might give me a drop out of your flask. I'm cold.

A. [*handing flask*]: Here you are.

B.: Listen! (2).

A.: What?

B.: I thought I heard something . . . up there . . .(3).

A.: You couldn't have. . . . What sort of sound?

B.: A kind of moaning, like a . . . There it is again!

A.: Yes, I heard that. . . . There must be something. We'd better go up and see (4).

B. [*clutching him*]: No!

NOTES

1. This scene should mount to a climax, A. gradually becoming affected by B.'s fear. There should at first be contrast between the two characters. B. is nervous and impressionable, and A. is comparatively confident and placid. B.'s movements should be fidgety, particularly his eyes. A.'s movements should be easy and smooth.

2. B. should pause in the act of raising the flask to his lips. Arrested action is always effective. (See page 25.)

3. It is effective to imagine the sound as coming from overhead, in the direction of the audience—perhaps in the top left-hand corner of the proscenium arch. The audience can then watch the direction of the two men's eyes as they stare upwards.

4. At the beginning of this speech. A. begins to show curiosity, which develops into anxiety, and something of B.'s fear. He rises and crosses B. to go out of the room, but B. catches him by the right arm as he passes. This movement needs careful timing.

EXERCISE 31

SCENE.—*A Room by moonlight or half-light.*

[A. *is an invalid in bed, or in a chair, covered with a rug, down* R. *There is a lamp beside him which lights up his face. There is a french window* C. B. *should appear silhouetted in this.*]

A.: What! You?

B.: Yes—me.

A.: What have you come for?

B. [*advancing to centre of room*]: Where is Elsa?

A.: Dead. You know that.

B.: Yes . . .

A.: Well, what do you want?

B.: I want you to die, too. I am going to kill you.

A.: You can't . . . you can't kill a man, ill . . . alone, and helpless . . .

B. [*advancing*]: Oh yes, I can . . . just as you killed Elsa.

A.: I did not kill her!

B.: She was alone and helpless—just like you . . . and she died slowly, painfully . . . something like this . . .

                          B. *smothers* A. *with the bedclothes.*

NOTE

This scene can be played in various ways, but B.'s part is more sinister if played very quietly throughout. A. should appear paralysed with fright, like a rabbit before a snake. Each of A.'s speeches should mount a further curve of climax, culminating in his fifth speech. His eyes should never leave B.'s face, and contracted movements of his hands are essential. Both should play for reserves. (See page 22.)

LOVE SCENES

Exercise 32

Scene.—*Any setting.*

[*Settee down* L. *Exit up* L.]

SHE: Do you love me, Paul?
HE: Of course I love you.
SHE: Kiss me (1).
HE: I must go now, my dear (2).
SHE: Good-bye, Paul.
HE: Good-bye. God bless you (3).

NOTES

Try playing this scene in two ways: (*a*) casually as in a sophisticated Coward-Lonsdale type of play; and (*b*) seriously and sincerely.

For (*a*) the girl could be lounging on the sofa, looking up at the man perched behind her on the back of it.

1. (*a*) He will lean over and kiss her lightly on the mouth.
2. (*a*) He will shake or pat her hand, casually.
3. He will speak these lines as he strolls to the door, blowing her a kiss as he goes out.

For (*b*) the two should be standing centre stage facing each other. She R., he L. Both profile to audience, their faces close to each other.

1. (*b*) She stands perfectly still as she says this, and then he puts his arms round her and kisses her passionately. Her weight must be towards him (see page 57). His right arm should be round her shoulders, and his left arm round her waist. Her arms are round his neck.

2. (*b*) They should come apart gradually on this line. Her hands should move slowly down his arms, until they reach his hands. They should stand for a moment, hands clasped.

3. (*b*) He should turn to go out after "Good-bye", and pause in the door to say "God bless you", then hurry out. Notice difference in timing of exit in (*a*).

EXERCISE 33

LOVE SCENE WITH CHANGE OF MOOD

SCENE.—*Any setting.*

[*Door or window* C. GIRL *sitting down* R. MAN *enters* C.]

HE: Mary!

SHE [*rising*]: Why have you come back? I told you I did not want to see you again.

HE: Won't you forgive me?

SHE: I have nothing to say to you.

HE: Mary!   [*They embrace.*

NOTE

This scene also should be played first (*a*) lightly, and then (*b*) seriously. In (*a*) the girl merely pretends to be angry, and the man is whimsical and coaxing. She capitulates finally into a laughing embrace.

In (*b*) the girl should keep her back turned to the man, who comes up behind her, and finally takes her forcibly by the shoulders, swings her round, and kisses her until she relents.

THE EFFECT OF MOOD ON SPEECH INFLEXIONS

Start here

EXERCISE 34

A.: Won't you let me explain?

B.: There's no need to explain. I think I understand.

A.: I felt sure you would.

B.: Why didn't you tell me about it at the time?

A.: I did not think it important enough to bother you about.

B.: Oh? . . . I am going now.

A.: When shall I see you again?

B.: I don't know.

NOTES

Try playing this scene in three different ways, and note how in each case inflexions, emphasis, and pace will be entirely different.

1. *As a love scene.* A., the man, is penitent and desperately eager to be forgiven. B., the woman, is hurt, tearful, and bewildered, uncertain whether to forgive him or not. The pace is fairly slow and halting.

2. *As a quarrel scene*, fast and furious, both are equally angry. A. is bitter and sarcastic on his second line.

3. *As a polite difference of opinion between business acquaintances.* A. is suave, coldly sarcastic, and in the right. B. is embarrassed, mortified, and in the wrong. A.'s utterance is smooth, precise, and measured. B.'s is alternately hasty and hesitating. Try this also with the positions reversed, B. being in the right.

end here

BURLESQUE

SCENE.—*Hall in a Castle.*

[*Doors* L. *and* R. KNIGHT *enters* R.]

KNIGHT: Stay there and guard the door. If any man try to enter, run him through with your sword.

SERVANT: Yes, my lord.

KNIGHT [*shouting*]: Ho there, Sir Bertram, come forth!

[*Enter* SIR BERTRAM, R., *munching gingerbread.*]

KNIGHT [*fiercely*]: Ah . . . at last! Seven days have I ridden full gallop by forest, field, and highway to rescue my sweet lady from your foul clutches, and now I have found you. Your serving-men lie slain without, my men-at-arms throng your courtyard, so you had better yield your prize to me. Where is the Lady Rosamund? [SIR BERTRAM *continues to munch, and jerks his head in the direction of the* U.L. *corner of stage.*]

KNIGHT: Bring her forth! [*Pause.*] I say, bring her forth —this instant, or I will cleave you where you stand, from top to toe.

SIR B. [*mouth full*]: Oh, don't do that.

KNIGHT: I will count ten, and if by then you have not delivered my lady safely into my arms you die.

SIR B.: Eh? What did you say?

KNIGHT [*irritated*]: You heard what I said. Now, I'm going to count—one, two, three, four, five, six, seven, eight, nine . . .

[*Enter* LADY ROSAMUND *knitting a stocking.*]

LADY R.: Oh Ronald, what a noise you are making. What's the matter?

KNIGHT: Matter? I have come to rescue you.

LADY R.: Oh, that . . . well, you'll have some dinner first with Bertram and me, won't you? I'll ring.

KNIGHT: They're all dead. . . . B-but don't you want to be rescued?

LADY R.: Well no, dear, not just now. You see Bertram and I have only been married a week. Now go along with Bertram and wash your hands for dinner.

KNIGHT: Well, but . . . oh, all right.

[*Exit with* SIR BERTRAM.

NOTES

Contrast should be maintained between the heroic ferocity of the Knight and the homeliness of Sir Bertram and the Lady. Sir Bertram should remain stolid and quite unmoved throughout the scene. The Knight's blustering manner begins to falter a little after Lady Rosamund's first speech, and he is completely deflated on his last speech, which should be spoken with perfectly natural and childish disappointment that the scene has not gone "according to plan".

CHARACTERIZATION

EXERCISE 36

SCENE.—*Any Interior.*

[MOTHER *sits down* L. ARCHIE *stands* C., *his back to the fireplace.*]

MOTHER: It's no good, Archie, nothing you say can make it any better (1). The disgrace of it! Really I feel quite ill . . . and I don't know what your father will say! He's paid for you to be educated like a gentleman, and now there you go, behaving like a common hooligan out of the streets! . . . My son appearing in the police-court for being drunk and disorderly . . . it's . . . it's . . . [*sobs*] I don't know *what* the Johnson-Smiths will think. . . .

ARCHIE: I'm terribly sorry, Mater; but you know what it is on boat-race night. Of course I'd no idea it would get into the papers.

MOTHER [*looking up*]: Papers? What papers?

ARCHIE: There's quite a big heading in the *Evening Standard*. [*Hands it to her.*]

MOTHER [*looking*]: Where?

ARCHIE: There.

MOTHER: This? (2). [*Reading.*] "Duke's son and friends in dock as a result of Undergraduate rag. Lord Hamish M'Donald, youngest son of the Duke of Dunfermline, Mr. Archibald Thompson, and the Hon. John Fitz-Allen appeared today . . ." My dear boy, why didn't you tell me? (3).

ARCHIE: Tell you what?

MOTHER: Why, that you were along with the son of a duke . . . [*Rises.*] Oh, my dear boy . . . [*kisses him*] . . . I mean . . . that's different. It will be a long time before the Johnson-Smiths see THEIR boy's name in the papers with a Duke's son (4). I must go and tell your father. [*Exit! calling off.*] Father. Have you seen that bit in the papers about our Archie and Lord Hamish M'Donald? . . .

NOTES

1. Be careful to point this line for "dramatic irony" and also the name "Johnson-Smiths" at the end of this speech.

2. The mother must appear puzzled at first as she reads this extract; enlightenment must come gradually and not completely till she comes to the words "Mr. Archibald Thompson".

3. A complete change in tone and manner is necessary at this point.

4. Comedy in this scene can only be achieved by contrast in manner and bearing, particularly on this line. The change

should be from a rather artificial dignity and refinement to frank homeliness, not unmixed with a certain spitefulness. The exit line should be spoken rapidly and shrilly.

5. Archie's attitude at the end of the scene can be either one of bewilderment, or may suggest that is saying to himself, "I thought as much".

EMOTIONAL ACTING

MEDIÆVAL PERIOD

EXERCISE 37

SCENE.—*The Hall of a Castle.*

[*Narrow window in wall* L. *Serving-men stand* L. *and* R. *of centre.* COUNT *standing up* L.C.]

[*Enter* MARCELLA.]

MARCELLA: What would you, my lord?

COUNT: Come here, Marcella (1). [*She approaches.*] Look through this grille (2). What see you down there?

MARCELLA: It is dim, my lord. I can see nothing.

COUNT: Look longer. Your eyes will grow accustomed to the gloom.

MARCELLA: I see a man, my lord, far below, crouching in the shadow, chained to the pillar. Now, I think he lifts his head.

COUNT [*to serving-man* L.]: Bring here a torch, and thrust it through the bars. [*Servant does so. A stifled gasp from* MARCELLA.] Know you that face, Marcella? (3).

MARCELLA: No, my lord. [*Turns away.*] (4).

COUNT: Turn not away (5). [*Holding her.*] See how the flame lights up his face. Is not that the face that last night lay pressed close to yours? Did not those fettered hands caress your bright hair? Did not those eyes look into yours last night, and those lips say "I love you"? Look well upon your lover, for by tonight that face shall want a pair of eyes wherewith to gaze upon you, and lack a tongue to utter passion's whisper. . . .

MARCELLA: You do not mean . . . (6). Take rather his life, and mine!

COUNT: This way better pleases me.

MARCELLA [*falling at his feet*]: My lord, have pity! I beg of you be merciful. . . .

COUNT [*to servant*]: Go, bid them heat the irons below.

[*Servant bows and exits up* L.

MARCELLA: O good, my lord, if you have human heart. . . . [*Rushes to grille.*] Belthane! Belthane! (7). [*Faints.*]

NOTES

1. The Count should keep very still and quiet at the beginning of the scene. (See note on Exercise 31.) He should use no gesture, but should command Marcella by voice and eye alone.

2. Marcella crosses in front of Count to window L.

3. Increase pace and tone on this line, and gradually throughout the Count's next speech.

4. This line may be said boldly and defiantly, or in a frightened undertone. The direction of the eyes is important here.

5. During this speech the Count should be standing behind Marcella, holding her by the shoulders, his face close to hers, but not masking it, both looking at the window, Marcella recoiling from it, but unable to escape. She must remember to breathe quickly throughout the Count's speech. This will help her to work up to her forthcoming hysterical outburst.

6. She breaks away from him here, and stands with her back to the window, leaning against it, and facing the Count.

7. The actress must not be afraid to let herself go at the end of this scene. The effect of hysteria in the voice is helped by letting out all the breath from the lungs, and forcing the voice

on a high note. The lack of breath will give the desired break in the voice.

REHEARSAL SCENE IN
CHARACTERIZATION AND REACTION

EXERCISE 38

"Art and the Woman"*

SCENE.—*A platform, and below it, in front, the backs of two rows of chairs are visible. The front row is empty and only a few people in second row.* PRESIDENT *in Chair,* SECRETARY *on her left.* SPEAKER *on her right, other committee members right and left.* CHAIRMAN *is standing.*

CHAIRMAN: I am very sorry to have to announce that Mrs. Jones is NOT the winner of the cake-making competition after all. Her entry was meringues, and the judges have decided that meringues are sweets and not cakes, and are therefore disqualified. So the prize goes to Mrs. Surtees for her Rock Buns. [*Applause and some cries of "Shame".*] Well, that concludes the business of the evening. And now, Fellow Members, I have much pleasure in introducing to you Mrs.—er—Miss Brenda Clare, who is going to give you a Demonstration in Mime . . . Meeme?

SPEAKER [*firmly*]: Mime.

CHAIRMAN: Yes, Mime. Now Miss Clare has kindly come

---

* *This sketch and all the exercises are fully protected by the law of copyright. No public performance may be given unless permission has been obtained in advance from Miss Frances Mackenzie. J. Garnet Miller Ltd., 13 Tottenham Street, London, W.1. The fee, which is 7s. 6d. for each public performance of the sketch, should be sent with the application for permission.*

to us from our Loamshire County Federation. [*Secretary nudges her and whispers.*] What? No? . . . Oh, of course, from London. Miss Clare has come all the way from London, and I know that we are all greatly looking forward to hearing her. . . .

SECRETARY [*prompting*]: Her book. . . .

CHAIRMAN: Ah yes. Miss Clare, as of course you know, is the author of that delightful little book, which I am sure we have all been reading and enjoying, called . . . er . . . [SECRETARY *hands paper*] called [*frowning at paper*] "Miming Games for Mothers".

SPEAKER: Mummers.

CHAIRMAN: What? Oh yes, Mummers. . . . Miss Deane, could you hand up my spectacles. I left them in my bag . . . on that chair . . . yes . . . there, with my knitting. Thank you so much. Yes, "Miming Games for Mummers". We have some copies, I think, on the table. . . . [SECRETARY *whispers.*] Oh, they have not come. . . .

SPEAKER: I happen to have a few copies with me if anyone wants to see it afterwards.

CHAIRMAN: Thank you, I'm sure we should. Well now, Miss Clare. . . .

[MISS CLARE *rises and advances, smiling, to front of platform, but a* MESSENGER *hurries in, agitated, and whispers to* CHAIRMAN *and* SECRETARY. SPEAKER *sits again. We overhear the words "Little Woodham" and "Oh dear" and "What shall we do?" Meanwhile about fifteen women arrive at door, up* L., *carrying bags, props, etc. Some are already made-up, one woman wears a beard under a "picture" hat. Some take their places noisily in front row, others line the wall at the left of the hall.*]

CHAIRMAN [*laughing nervously*]: Well now, Fellow Members, such an awkward thing has happened. Little Woodham Institute have just arrived to give us their play. I am afraid, owing to some mistake, we gave them the wrong date. Actually we expected them at our *next* monthly meeting, 26th November. . . . But— here they all are. . . . I wonder . . . How long does your demonstration take, Miss Clare?

SPEAKER: About an hour and a half.

CHAIRMAN: Oh dear, and it is now a quarter-past eight. Perhaps South Woodham . . . Mrs. Forester, would you come up here? [*She comes.*] Mrs. Forester is the South Woodham President. Do you think that you could give us your little play AFTER Miss Clare's talk, Mrs. Forester? What play is it?

MRS. FORESTER: *King Lear.*

CHAIRMAN: N-not the whole of *King Lear?*

MRS. FORESTER: We have cut some scenes. It lasts about two and a half hours.

CHAIRMAN: . . . Oh, then in that case . . . I'm afraid we shall HAVE to ask you to come to us next month instead, 26th November.

A COMMITTEE MEMBER: You asked me to give a talk that day on "Forty Ways of Using Feathers and Farm Refuse".

CHAIRMAN: Well, perhaps, Miss Rust, as you live in the district . . . I think we must go into that later. . . . I'm sure South Woodham are so pleased to have this opportunity of hearing Miss Clare, aren't you? [*Dead Silence, One voice says "No". Some applause.*] Yes, I'm sure you are. We must all remember our Golden Thread for this Month, "Endurance". So now, Miss Clare. . . .

SPEAKER [*rising*]: Ladies and . . . ladies. I am so very glad to have this opportunity of talking to you on a subject . . .

[*Black out.*]

VOICE IN DARKNESS: It's only the lights.

SECRETARY'S VOICE: Do you think you could carry on if I held a flash-light in front of you?

SPEAKER: No.

CHAIRMAN'S VOICE: Keep your seats, Members, keep your seats.

VOICE: Isn't there a MAN anywhere about?

CURTAIN

NOTE ON THE CHARACTERS

Chairman. The success of the entire scene depends on the playing of this part, whose personality must dominate and control it throughout. The effect of the scene is to a great extent that of a long speech from the Chairman, punctuated by frequent interruptions, which must never be allowed to hold up the pace of the scene. This requires good team work from the minor characters, for if the comedy gets out of hand it will fail. The Chairman must have a good sense of timing. There are several ways in which the part might be played, varying with the personality of the player. She can be made either good-natured and charming, but hopelessly vague and flustered, or she could be blandly casual and off-hand. There must be a dominating quality in the voice of this player.

Speaker. Bored, impatient, but assumes a professional "brightness" every time she rises to begin her lecture.

Secretary. Quiet, prompt, efficient.

Mrs. Forester. Grim, uncompromising, and definitely "highbrow". A deep voice is essential.

Miss Rust. "Touchy" and difficult, but too nervous to stand her ground.

N.B.—The comedy of a scene of this type will not get over if it is played too broadly. The characters must not be "guyed", and, above all, the audience must never be allowed to feel that the actors are conscious of their own humour. (See page 37.)